# the good braider

### a novel

## terry farish

SKYSCAPE

No part of this publication may be reproduced,
stored in a retrieval system, or transmitted, in any form or
by any means, electronic, mechanical, photocopying, recording, or otherwise,
without the prior permission of the copyright owner. Request for permission should be addressed to
the Publisher, Amazon Publishing, Attn: Amazon Children's Publishing, P.O. Box 400818,
Las Vegas, NV 89140, www.amazon.com/amazonchildrenspublishing

This book is a work of fiction. Names, characters, places, and incidents are products of the author's imagination and
are used fictitiously. Any resemblance to actual events or locales or persons, living or dead, is entirely coincidental.

Library of Congress Cataloging-in-Publication Data

Farish, Terry.
The Good braider / by Terry Farish. – 1st ed.
p. cm.
Summary: Follows Viola as she survives brutality in war-torn Sudan, makes
a perilous journey, lives as a refugee in Egypt, and finally reaches
Portland, Maine, where her quest for freedom and security is hampered by
memories of past horrors and the traditions her mother and other Sudanese
adults hold dear. Includes historical facts and a map of Sudan.
ISBN 978-1-4778-1628-8 (paperback) – ISBN 978-0-7614-6267-5 (hardcover) – ISBN 978-0-7614-6268-2 (ebook)
[1. Refugees–Fiction. 2. Immigrants–Fiction. 3. Sudanese
Americans–Fiction. 4. Mothers and daughters–Fiction. 5.
Sudan–History–Civil War, 1983-2005–Fiction. 6. Portland (Me.)–Fiction.]
I. Title.

PZ7.F22713Goo 2012
[Fic]–dc23


2011033659

Xuân Huong, excerpt from "Spring-Watching Pavilion," translated by
John Balaban, from *Spring Essence: The Poetry of H Xuân Huong*.
Copyright © 2000 by John Balaban. Reprinted with the permission of
The Permissions Company, Inc., on behalf of Copper Canyon Press,
www.coppercanyonpress.org.

Excerpt from CROW AND WEASEL by Barry Lopez, with illustrations by
Tom Pohrt. Text Copyright © 1990 by Barry Holstun Lopez. Reprinted
by permission of North Point Press, a division of Farrar, Straus and Giroux, LLC.

*Book design by Anahid Hamparian and Sonia Chaghatzbanian*
*Editor: Melanie Kroupa*

SKYSCAPE

the good braider

For Angela, Suzan's baby daughter.
May you grow up with hope in the birth of South Sudan
and thrive in America, your home.

And for Melanie

"The spirit of Africa . . . always appears
in the guise of an elephant."

—Ryszard Kapuściński, *The Shadow of the Sun*

# Fire

I run breathless into my house.
What will I tell her?
I will tell her, *Andrew has my book.*
The teacher assigned us to work together.
But my mother does not turn to me.
She wears her after-work clothes,
her African dress that hangs
loose from her shoulders.
Maybe she has not seen me with Andrew—
my friend—seen me leap from his truck.
I watch the bend of her shoulders.
She holds herself rigid and does not
look at me. I'll leave here again when the families
from Juba come to eat and watch news of the war.
I turn and look toward the door.
As if she can read my mind, she commands,
"You will stay in this house!"
*She knows.*
She knows I have been away from our people.
I have slipped out of Africa for a breath of time.
Do my hair and my skin smell different?
I pause at the kitchen doorway.
She turns, and her eyes are ferocious.
I watch the water bubble up.
In Juba, the pot would need huge flames
to build the water to this boil.
I step toward my mother and the boiling water.

I mean to take the spoon and stir while the *aseeda*
thickens in the boiling water, this dense white food
that to our Sudanese people is life.
Instead I say, "Sometimes I do not want to know
how many people have died in the war."
I say this
as the aseeda bubbles loudly
over the red electric coils.
Maybe it is those words
that cause what happens next.
She grabs my arm. She holds it hard
by my wrist and my elbow.
She twists my hand over the steam.

"*Yumis*, Mother! You are hurting me!"

*Now the war comes back to me.*

*Again, there is only the war.*

# Part One
## *Elephant Bone*

Africa

Juba, Sudan, and Cairo, Egypt

1999–2002

# Be Free

I hear Congolese music playing ahead
of me on the dusty road.
The *tcha tcho* music says, *Be free.*
I hear it over the roar
of the war planes that choke the sky.
My body wants to sway and my hips want to circle
and my arms want to rise above my head
and let go of my jerry can of water.
The music comes from a building
made of metal sheets, and in the doorway
stands a boy.
I know him.
I feel my body soften.
He is a Bari like me,
not like the government soldiers
from the northern part of Sudan
who surround us.
The boy steps into the road ahead of me,
and I see his narrow back.
The ball of sun falling
behind us
makes his back glisten.
*Hurry,* my mother told me. *Bring the water.*
*Talk to no one.* But I can't stop looking at the boy's
narrow back. I hear my mother,
*Soldiers put you in jail for talking to a boy.*
I know this. I walk.

In Juba you're not supposed to show
your legs if you are on the road.
I tuck my skirt around my ankles
so the Muslim soldiers do not believe
I am a crime against God.
In the zigzags between my braids
the sun pierces the back of my scalp.
The boy turns. His eyes flash to mine
and away. I move my thigh almost but not quite
in step with his, as if we can outstep this war.
He slows. I glance sideways at him.
Keeping him in my gaze,
I walk to his rhythm of freedom,
as if we have a right to imagine,
as if the government soldiers
who occupy our city
value the life of the people of southern Sudan.

The drums beat *Be free.*
I want to tell this boy,
"I have an uncle in Maine, America,
if you want to talk about freedom."
This boy has no freedom here.
At any second the army can say,
*Boy! I have a use for you.*
Still, I imagine the boy talking low and deep,
*When freedom comes,*
*I am going to love the beautiful girls*
*of southern Sudan.*
I move my body
to the drums. I imagine we are free.

The boy and I walk in paths side by side,
though he stays a step before me.
He turns.
This time, though, his eyes dart
to a movement behind me and widen.
I look quickly.
I see a light-skinned soldier,
his boots wiping out my footprints in the dust.
He has a black front tooth.
"*Salaam alaikum,*" I say almost silently. *Peace to you.*
His *perik* falls down his back, quiet now,
but in the night I know its scream of fire.
Four bullets in a single second.
*Prrrrrrrrrrrrrrrrrrr.*
Dead.
Soldiers come before the sun rises if they suspect
you are a friend with the rebels.
"*Ahlen,*" replies the soldier. *Welcome.*
But he does not leave my footsteps.
His boot cuts into my heel.
I even smell his tobacco—
a sweet kind of molasses odor.
*Run,*
I tell myself.
But I hesitate.
We're still near the building that rocks
with drums. My mother's words warn me:
*Use your head. Are you faster than a gun?*
Then I hear the voice of the boy
with the narrow back.
"She is my sister," the boy says,

turning, standing tall. "She is young."
In some place other than Juba,
a brother
might prevent what is to happen.
Our feet—his and mine—stop in the dust,
sinking into our own burning footprints.
I see a flash of terror
in his eyes,
and I am awed that he would do this,
call out, on the street,
when we both . . .

The soldier lifts his perik.
The boy spins, runs like a gazelle.
*No!* I cry out loud.
The blast
fills my ears.
*Prrrrrrrrrrrrrrrrr*
*Mother!*
Is all I think.

Now, I am running.
Dust flies around me. I glance back
toward the place
where the boy fell.
He lies still, his arms thrown wide across the dirt
for saying, *She is young. She is my sister.*
For trying to protect me,
the daughter of a rebel soldier.
My eyes jerk from the hollow of the boy's back

to the soldier with the black tooth who smells like
tobacco
and molasses.
My legs shake, barely holding me. Water slops down my body.
But the soldier slings the rifle on his shoulder.
He is in no hurry with me.
I walk to the water tap every day.

# Girl from Juba

*"You did not know him?"*
*"Yes, we know him."*
*"He is from Yei."*
*"I know his mother."*
*"How do you know you know his mother?"*
*"Any boy in Juba, Tereza thinks she knows."*

Women are gathered in our courtyard with my
mother, called Tereza, my grandmother, Habuba,
and my little brother, Francis.
They talk about this latest killing.
Kiden, my little cousin, sits between my knees.
My fingers shake in her hair,
which I'm supposed to be dressing.
Kiden reaches up and pretends to braid mine.
I feel her tiny fingers poke and see her wide
eyes, her eyelashes almost touching mine.
I twist a bit of red and yellow cloth and tie it quick
like a band around her head.

Some mothers and their children have fled
here—to Juba—from their villages.
Other mothers have fled to the
refugee camps. That is what they talk about:
how to flee.

Women come to our courtyard for my mother's braids.
When I was young my little fingers
rode on her long narrow ones.

Her fingers danced over my cousins' hair like feathers,
shaping twists and lines with a single tiny bead
slipped on the end.
I learned to braid by feel more than sight.
My mother calls me by two names, Viola, for Jesus,
and Keji, for firstborn girl.
"All men in Sudan will want to marry you," she used to say.
"You are a girl from Juba."

I listen to my grandmother and the mothers talk.
My mother tells of my uncle Marko in America,
but she shakes her head in fear.
"They get killed on the way,
the people who run. It is a long way.
No one is on the side of the women . . ."
She gestures to take in all the soldiers
from the north who occupy our city.
"Not them or the rebels."
The rebels are our people of the south.
But our southern tribes fight each other
and would kill a child for his food.
Francis takes this cue to march and sing
the SPLA rebel song:

> *Even your mother, give her a bullet.*
> *Your gun is your food. Your gun is your wife.*

*"Shut that boy up."*
*"It is only a song to him. He doesn't know."*
*"They will come for him soon enough."*

I grab Francis and drag him over to Kiden and me.

We have listened, breathless, to stories.
One family walked from their village to Kenya,
all the way to Kakuma Refugee Camp.
Most who try it will die.
In the bush outside of Juba there is
bombing, bombing, bombing.
People used to escape by barge up the Nile,
but now the government in the north
controls the barges. A few lucky ones escape
on the plane to Khartoum, but to get on the passenger list,
you must know someone high up.
I do not speak.
I listen
and think of the boy with the narrow back.


"Pulling hard and tight does not make a braid
last," my mother instructed when I was young.
"Narrow rows make them last.
Braid three strands,
Two together, lift a strand from the side.
Two together, lift a strand from the side.
Narrow!"


Sometimes it takes five or six hours to braid.
When I was little I listened to the women talk—
*"Eat the soil from the Nile to make your blood strong.*
*Braid your hair well, or no one will marry you.*
*Rub the man's feet when he comes home.*

*Never serve lumpy aseeda. He will leave you.*
*Be clever. Be quick-tongued.*
*Even then he may take a bride in Uganda."*
My mother taught me to stir the aseeda,
stitch the clothes, braid the hair.
I learned these tasks to increase my bride price.


The women leave our courtyard, many with little
food to cook for the evening meal.
My grandmother and I sweep the straw mats
on the floor. Even our house feels like a prison.
Among the people who were here,
could anyone doubt what we must do?
*Flee*
for our freedom.
I say this to my mother.
"It is not so easy, Keji." She does not look at me.
"What keeps us here?" I say.
"When did you get so rich!" my mother snaps,
"that you can ask such a question. We have to pay
at every step of the way. How do you
think we will eat?"
I would rather escape than eat,
but children do *not* disagree with their parents.
Francis runs to our mother,
wraps his arms around her neck.
We hear the roar of government planes.
Outside the city perimeter, the rebels,
barefoot and hungry,

amass stockpiles of weapons.
Still, my grandmother says,
"Maybe Keji is right.
Maybe it is time."

# Elephant Bone

When it's dark and the power has gone off,
my mother presses something hard into my palm.
I can't see it, but she says it's a bit of elephant
bone she found among the stones farther north
on the Nile. "It's good luck," she says.
"No animal can kill the elephant."
I wrap my fingers around it.
Once she told me about an elephant she saw—
ten feet tall, swinging its tail in play,
and splashing in the river.
She saw an elephant lie for days
with its trunk across the wide shoulder
of another who was dying.
She says, "They lift their trunks
and cry. It is like they are singing,
and the song
goes on
for hundreds of verses."
Maybe we are family, me and the elephants.

"I am talking to the relatives," my mother whispers,
as if soldiers can hear us. I know if you know
somebody who knows somebody,
sometimes an Arab merchant will let you talk
on his phone to your family in America.
Maybe Uncle Marko can help us to escape.

# Gwendolyn's Garden

My neighbor is seventeen.
She is a widow, like most of the married girls.
She goes by Gwendolyn, her Jesus name,
and is the only person with a garden.
When the soldiers seized Juba,
they planted landmines where sorghum and kale
used to grow in the fields beyond the city.
Now we are surrounded by a ring of death.
Cornmeal, lentils, and sometimes oil for cooking
from the UN food station are our only foods.
Many have tried to pray something green out of the
dust by our houses, but only Gwendolyn makes shoots
rise from the earth.
I wake up thinking about Gwendolyn's garden.
I find myself in front of her house
when the sun comes up.
I crouch down to her fragile green stalks.
Groundnuts.
The best Gwendolyn can do.
If I could coax groundnuts from the dirt like this,
we'd have groundnuts to sell.
Money when we flee.

I find Gwendolyn by her fire, stirring porridge.
I crouch beside her. "If I keep your plants watered,
would you give me some shells for seeds?"
Her belly bulges with baby.

She says, "It's hard bringing the water."
So we agree.
Francis finds me studying Gwendolyn's garden.
His lips spread in a smile. "What?" I say.
"Play the moon game," he cries.
He likes to make up ways for us to touch the moon.
"Do you want to go by donkey?" I tease.
"Help me. Open your hands."
He raises his hands and his little palms cup
the shells Gwendolyn drops there.
"I want to climb a groundnut vine to the moon."
"You are silly," I say.
"You are silly, too," he says.
Gwendolyn rests her tired face against her hand
and smiles at us.

We hoe the dusty soil outside our courtyard.
We plant a dozen fragile seeds
in narrow rows two inches deep.
Very slowly, the plants will sprout
and send shoots to grow in fragile knots.
The knots produce pods,
and when the pods have veins,
it will be time to harvest.
Can we wait that long, to have groundnuts to sell?

# Daughter's Work

I hold the plastic jug by my side
and stand by Habuba.
"I am going to the tap," I say.
Habuba knows trouble is on this path.
She lifts an empty plastic jug.
"We will do the daughter's work together."
We both know any soldier on our way can do
what he likes. "I will go with you," she says again.
We walk.
She tells me stories—about the chicken
who used to roost under a basket,
how the acacia tree used to shade the courtyard.
All my life I've been here in this dust city.
I bathed in the Nile but
never crossed into the bush,
never saw the lion or the chicken.
They even had to close my school
because it wasn't safe to send the children.
With bright cloths Habuba and I have covered
our heads from the sun,
as if this were a different time,
as if we are simply
two women
going for water.

# Daughter Dreaming

The relatives come and, while I cook in the kitchen,
I hear the hum
of worried women.
My job is to cook
and wash the pots,
laying them on the wire cage where
the chickens used to sleep. I stir the pot of aseeda.
I have made all Habuba's memories my own—
the sweet smell of cinnamon tea, the swaying acacia,
the sharp crow of the rooster. Scoops of sugar
in her tea.  My father brought us a tin of sweetened
condensed milk. I hardly knew him,
but I remember the sweet milk. We heated it for our tea.
Ohhh, I loved that tea! But it's been five years
since then, the year Francis was born.

I stir the aseeda, but in my mind
I am somewhere else.
I want to live the stories Habuba tells.
Suddenly, I want *out* of here.
In my mind I own a chicken like Habuba did.
In my mind I dance to Congolese music.
Then I remember the boy and the *tcha tcho* music,
*Be free.*
It pounds in my head. I want to escape
our kitchen, where I spend every night cooking
and cleaning pots, afraid tonight
the soldiers will break into our house.

I dream of America, where Uncle Marko lives.
I dream of the boy's long back
and how his arms framed his body.
I dream of his hands
touching my face and my twisty braids.
I dream of *freedom*
and move to the sound in my head of Congolese drums.

My mother comes.
She stares at the pot I am supposed to be stirring.
I look. Aseeda blackens the bottom.
You do not disobey your mother.
Her wide strong hand
slaps me hard across my jaw.
The sudden, sharp pain splits my body from my mind.
I fall against the wall.
"Why aren't you stirring?" I hear my mother's voice.
Slowly, I return to my body and this kitchen.
"I was thinking," I whisper.
I turn to her. I do not protect my face.
She is teaching me to never question what she says to do.
If you stop to question, then, when the bombs come,
you will die.
My mother shakes her head.
"Pay attention," she commands.

Francis squats beside me and helps me
turn the spoon in the aseeda that is now getting stiff.
Then my little brother runs back out to play.
I stir. I stop my dreams of dancing and chickens.

I return to this world: the hum of worried voices
from the courtyard. I go to the door to listen.
*"They bombed the school in Yei."*
*"The children ran into the bush."*
*"No mother will allow her child to go to school again."*
The school!
I sink into the door.
I think of my school and how I miss it.
I miss the rows of desks and thin-papered books.
Kiden and Francis never got to go to school—
even for a single day.

I take water left from the cooking
and pour half over the dirt where I planted the seeds.
With the jug half full, I walk under the moon
to Gwendolyn's garden,
where her seeds sprout like whiskers.
My head pounds from the blow to my jaw
and the guess that we can't wait
for these groundnuts
to burst.

# No Escape

"*Come.*"
In Gwendolyn's garden, his voice pierces the dark.
A soldier.
I can't see him. But I know!
I begin to run. I don't know which way.
The cloth I wear in the kitchen over my skirt
is coming untied. I trip.
I rip it from my hips and run.
Laughter riddles his throat
like the rounds of his *perik*.
"No other rebels here," the soldier says softly.
He comes out on the road
in the beginning moonlight.
I see Francis run past the sandbags
that line the opposite side of the road.
Francis must not come closer.
He must not cross the road,
give himself away.
*I* must not give him away.
I warn Francis with a rigid shake of my head.
A scream begins in my belly,
but there is Francis. I have stopped
breathing. Brother, do not call out *Keji*!
He starts to run toward me with the mango
he's been using for a kicking stone.
My eyes warn him, *no*!
The soldier is close enough to touch me now.

The same black-toothed man who killed the boy.
He shifts his rifle.
Five-year-old Francis holds still.
My mother taught us both well—
*Always do what the mother says.*
Now I am the mother.
If he even begins to cry . . .
The sight of the soldier's long, unshaven
throat makes me nauseous. In that second I fear I will
die from the pounding of my heart.
The soldier waves his perik, his chin in the air.
I smell the sickening sweet tobacco.
"Come!" he says again.
No! My body warns my little brother whom I no longer
dare to look at. He is so close that in my mind
I see "Magic Kingdom,"
the words on his best T-shirt from the UN.
The soldier kicks his perik against my back.
"Come!" he says.
"Please," I say. "My mother is waiting."
"I will come for her next," he says.
I imagine his thin, straight smile.
I suck in my breath.
My body quivers against the muzzle of the gun.
Francis stands—wide-legged—across the road,
waiting.
*Do not move. Wait for me here.*
The soldier looks at my brother.
When his eyes turn to me they speak clearly,
*You know we take boys to be soldiers.*

I don't hesitate again.
I follow the soldier.

In my mind, I hold the picture of my brother.
I need to walk back out and see my brother.
*I will not die.*
The soldier slams me into the dirt.
*I will not die.*
The sickening tobacco smell penetrates my nose,
my lungs, the skin between my legs.
"If you cry out, I will kill you," he says.
I am crushed into the red earth and
do not know if this is alive or dead, this place
where there is only ripping pain.

I am sorry, Yumis.
Please . . . forgive me, my mother.

Francis is still there,
his worried eyes on the wait-a-bit,
what we call the prickly shrub at the bend
of the path where I had disappeared from him.
I am aware of the curve of his shoulders.
He holds the empty plastic jug in which I carried the
water for the groundnuts.
I had dropped it in the road. I imagine the water
soaking into the dust.
*I did not die.* I am hunched and hobble toward him.
I take Francis's tiny hand and somehow
in my mind, I confuse the water for the groundnuts

that covers the path
with the blood of the boy who called me *sister*
to save me.
Then I let Francis lead me home.

# Palm Oil

At home I rub palm oil in my mother's hair.
She is silent.
She knows. Everybody knows.
The story rolls along like drumbeats
from house to house.
*Viola has lost her bride wealth.*
I am gentle and divide her hair.
My mother cries.
I braid lines to the nape of her neck.
"I will send you away," she says.
I do not talk back.
I wipe the tears from her nose.
The lines of her braids are tiny and too tight.
"Why were you on the road at *night?*"
Her words are like knives.
"What kind of *girl* would be on the road at *night?*
You have brought us shame."
It *wasn't* night when I went. I don't say this.
I know I have brought her terrible shame.
Dreaming of groundnuts and money.
I am panting with terror
and the realization that I could so easily be dead.
And my brother.
I whisper, "Do you remember the elephant bone?"
My mother scowls but nods yes.
I want her to be glad she gave me its strength.
I rest my head against her chest. *Comfort me,*

I want to say.
I want her to tell me I am still her child.

I do not say this—she knows—
that he pressed the perik into my cheek.
Earth clods cut my skin.
I smelled oil and metal,
the soldier's tobacco smell.
The hand ripped me open,
then the whole iron man.
I wrenched my body
across the dirt. His mouth sucked my breath.
I knew soon the butt of his perik would slam
into my head.
But then the elephant appeared to me.
*Be still,* she warned.

I finish braiding my mother's hair.
Now we both smell of palm oil.
I sit beside her, my bony shoulder pressed to hers.
I am taller than she is. Almost six feet.
My heart seems to have dropped between my legs
and beats against my bloody thighs.
"Don't forget to take the quinine," she says.
A long exhale escapes from my belly.
"I always take the quinine," I whisper.
Everyone takes quinine when the malaria comes.
But my mother is thinking of the large dose
to stop a baby. "Don't forget," she orders.
I pull a leather pouch from my pocket,

worn soft like a baby's belly.
It had belonged to my father.
It fits in my palm.
I slide the zipper and show her one hundred piasters.
Five small coins.
They are filthy, but on each we see a cow,
the symbol of wealth.
She glances at them. She does not speak.
She does not ask me where I got them,
and I will never tell her.
But I know in her head she has already spent them.

# Quinine

I am swollen three times, four times,
the flesh there.
I am bloody, and that part of me has become
the center of my body.
It throbs when I walk
and in my dreams.
When I wake I smell tea and see a cup
placed on the shelf. Habuba would do this.
The tea is thick and black,
strong Kenyan tea she mysteriously acquired.
Beside it is a gourd holding tablets of quinine.
I think Habuba has given me her own
and scrounged up more. A girl I know took twelve,
but still a baby came. I sit cross-legged on my mat
with the strong brewed tea and force the tablets down.
*Achhhhh*, I gag at the bitterness.
I wash the acrid taste from my tongue with the tea.
I focus on not vomiting them up. I will *not*
let the quinine rise back up and burn my throat
I will defy the soldier with quinine. With *health*.
I swallow . . . and swallow,
staring down his black eyes with revenge in mine.
*I spit spit spit on you!*

Later, Francis climbs on my mat with me.
"Are you sleeping?"
His small hands touch my face.

"We might go on a journey," he whispers.
"I don't care," I say.
"Habuba says we can eat chocolate in America."
He blows the word *chocolate* on my eyelids.
I throb and curve around my monster body.
A thought frightens me:
What if my mother leads
everyone on the airplane
and I am left, bound to the war?

# Daughter of Experience

I sleep again from sunrise until the afternoon.
When I wake, I feel a large gray stillness with me,
all that is left from a dream: an elephant dream.
I know it is the elephant who came
when the soldier took me.
The image sways, and when I wake up,
I wake to the pounding of rotors of government
gunships. There is only the war.
I wrap my arms around myself.

Habuba stands in the doorway.
"Did you sleep?" she asks.
I nod yes.
"Did you dream?"
I still feel the rhythm.
"I remember an elephant," I say.
"That is a good dream," she says.
"Who follows the elephant will have no problems.
They know how to make a path through the forest."
We sit in the courtyard.
Her thick fingers encircle a gourd
filled with thin porridge.
She places it in my palms.
Then she slips her hand into a cloth bag
and pulls out seven red glass beads.
They roll in her palm, and the sun dances
through them. With the movement of a finger,

she motions for me to sit at her feet.
She also produces a gold-colored rag
that she rips into strips. "I will dress your hair,"
she says. I sit where she says. I close my eyes.
Soon, I feel her fingers twisting my hair.
It barely hurts,
but tears wash
through my closed eyes and spill onto my shirt.
Habuba begins to talk.
She misses the trees that surrounded Juba
when she was young, the tamarind, the acacias,
the dense forest, the shoebill bird in the swamp.
She misses weavers in the woods.
"Even the trees and birds don't find life in Juba."
Her fingers cross round the crown of my head,
squeezing out the tears.
She weaves the strips of gold rag into my hair.
"Once there was a man who wanted to die," she says,
"but he was told it is death's job to do the taking.
Death is not looking for you, Viola," Habuba says.
"You have things to do. God gave you long legs
for walking and running."
She turns me and runs her callused hand
down my legs to my rubber flip-flops
and the tall arch of my big feet.
"You are a daughter with a quick mind
who learns fast from experience.
You'll learn a tongue gives you power."
She grips my face hard, and her fingers press

the long bones that run across my cheeks
and then she clasps me by the ears.
"Here you are sensitive because you listen
and remember, even the things you want to forget."
She takes up the beads one by one.
She places the end of one braid
between the open ends of a hairpin.
She presses the hairpin through the hole in the bead.
She threads the bead onto my braid.
One dances over the side of my forehead,
just by my left eye. When she is done,
I look at my reflection in a shard of mirror.
I find a girl who looks solemn in the eyes.
I see thick quarter moons for eyebrows.
I see round, determined lips.
But her hair, this girl's hair, springs out
in knots of gold. The sun shimmers
through the red beads.
I look in the mirror and watch that girl.
with the round, unsmiling, sure lips.
She still wants to be free.
I think of Francis . . .
and again
of America.

# Dawn

I startle awake in the courtyard.
It is hot even before the sun rises.
I feel the night's heat against my body
that still throbs. Francis sleeps beside me.
Silence. I listen. I can't see my mother's eyes,
but I know she is awake and listening, too,
for footsteps.
We lie together in one bed, knotted, breathing.


Marko has relayed to my mother
news about the UN cargo plane.
He says flying in it is nothing to worry about.
The hard part is getting on the list. We will sit
on the plane's floor, packed with hundreds of others,
and rise above the trees. He is working on the hard part,
the list. He relays that he knows a priest who knows
an employee of the UN.
If Marko can get our names on the list to escape
like cargo, we would fly to Khartoum, the capital
in northern Sudan.
Somehow on land and water get to Cairo,
to get refugee status and then—maybe—
to America.
I cannot imagine stepping into one of the planes
whose engine roar has terrified us all our lives.

The voices of the women only warn:
"Impossible," they say, "to walk away from Juba
through the perimeter of landmines."
"Get on the list if you can," they say.
But how long can we wait?
Some people, though, can no longer tolerate
the constant terror of the soldiers, the stealing
of the children, the hunger.
They will take any risk to leave.
Last night, my mother counted the coins
in the leather purse. If she pays a rebel soldier
and he guides us through the forest,
maybe we could escape to a refugee camp
to the south,
to Kenya.

# Food

As the north Sudanese soldiers suspect,
my mother has friends among the rebels.
She knows Jacob. He is old and maybe fled himself
from the SPLA rebel army. But he says he has passed
through the minefields. Not just once.
Many times. And look at him. Hasn't he lived to tell it?
He'll guide us out of Juba. He knows a path clear of mines
and starving rebels who would ambush us.
None of us is sure what Jacob really knows,
but he knows more than us.
We will be ready. If the time comes,
we will be ready.

Our first step: Habuba and I wait in the food line
in the sun to collect rations.
We wait for two hours and finally it is our turn.
They are not out of all food as they often are.
Quickly we fill our bags. I balance a sack of beans.
Habuba carries dusty powdered milk. Plane engines roar
from the government airfield. We turn. I look only at
boots of soldiers as we walk. The closer I am to home,
all the boots become the boots of *that* soldier.
I want to run.
Habuba grabs my arm.
"Walk," she commands.
"A few more steps."
I walk. We have passed!

We run the final steps, stumble into the house,
deposit the food on the ground, and somehow laugh
at ourselves for our success.
But then my grandmother says she is very tired.
She eases herself down to rest in the courtyard.
We are tense and nervous, yet still we are laughing.
I sit beside her. Lately she hasn't had her same strength.
But Habuba lets out a single, high-pitched sound in
excitement, then flings her hands over her mouth. I say,
"If we go to America, we can sing as loud as we want."
Tears fill her eyes, and I know she is scared, too.
"Habuba," I say, "am I a child? I mean in America,
would I be a child? Because if I am a child,
maybe I can go to school. I know English." A little.
We studied English in a mission school
until the government forbade it.
*Only Arabic*, the government ordered.

"You will be a child," Habuba says.
I want to hug every bone of her.
Something that feels like drumbeats
pounds into my fingers and my toes.
I will go to school and dig for the English
inside my head.

# Thyme

In three days, when leaving still seems
like a fantasy, my mother commands, "Get ready.
You must pack everything on your body."
Habuba and I prepare okra and the wide flat *kisra*
and wrap the food in cloth.
"Pray to Jesus to protect you,"
Habuba says over and over.
My fingers are clumsy as I shape the bread.
This is the longest day.
And something is not right with Habuba.
She watches me too much.
She teases me. Once she stops work and rests her arms
around my shoulders and presses her forehead to mine.
Every minute we pray not to hear the soldiers'
boots approach our house.
Finally
the ball of sun begins to drop.
Habuba brings out the thyme oil she keeps in a tiny bottle,
and when she dabs the oil on the insides of my elbows,
I smell like her.
Then she gives me a small package.
"Why are you giving this to me?" I say.
"It is our only book. If you study,
you can bring more than a bride's wealth."
She narrows her eyes.
The book is her hymnal in our mother tongue, Bari.
"You can be a teacher."

Her eyes gleam. "Maybe it is tonight. Maybe not yet.
But now you are ready!" In the dark, she straps rations
to my chest and belly. It is as if she is pushing me
on my way. But then my mother calls,
and I have to leave her.

In fits and starts,
my mother hums the hymns we know.
She does this to calm herself
while she stirs the stew, the job she wants me to take.
My mother loves to sing the Jesus songs.
Francis sits on his haunches and stares at her.
It's like he's holding his breath while she hums,
waiting for her to finish a line.
We all know the words we aren't singing:

> *That's why I pray to you in the morning.*
> *That's why I pray to you in the evening.*
> *That's why I pray to you in the night time.*
> *That's why I pray to you all the time.*

She begins to hum another line . . .
and stops short
when we
hear a sound on the road.
The sound of boots.
"Run!" my mother commands.
Habuba grabs Francis in her arms.
They run.
But I will not leave my mother.

# Last Offer

The soldier lights a cigarette
and leans against our courtyard wall.
We rise from the cook fire.
My mother tries to hide me,
but at the slight lift of his chin,
we freeze.
Vomit rises in my throat.
My mother holds me. I know what will happen
if I run.
We lower our heads.
If he touches me,
he will feel the rations strapped
to my stomach.
He will shoot us all
and walk away, smoking.
I can see his long, thin throat,
smell his reek of spoiled onion
and tobacco.
I lean toward the pot.
Not breathing.
"I brought you some sugar," the soldier says softly,
his eyes not leaving my face until he
thrusts a full kilo sack into my mother's chest.
I am falling but I think of my grandmother's voice:
*You are strong.*
I force my legs to hold me.
This offer is an old trick.

All my people know.
This promise from his smooth, slick tongue.
Always a promise—sugar, grain to a starving
southern Sudanese. We know this trick.
*Just become Muslim,* they mean.
*You will never be hungry again if you are Muslim.*
If we take the sugar, he will own us.
He knows.
We know.
The soldier says, "Treat yourself.
You have no sugar.
Take it," he says. "Then come to prayers."
We need only to pray
with the Muslim women.
The soldier shows the black tooth when he grins.
My mother's mouth is set. I know she wants
to spit at him. Even now she'd do this.
I hold my breath.
She lays the sugar at his boot.
He slides his perik from his back and into
his arms
and aims it at my face.
My mother is a statue beside me.
I clasp her ribs.
He does not shoot but laughs
at me
as he turns his back.

I know he will return, as long as I am here.
For some minutes,

after he is out of sight
we do not move.
Then my muscles give way.
I kneel in the dirt.
My mother kneels, too.
My mother's arms and legs are strong around me,
and then we rise
as if we are one person.

# Go!

We race,
taking only what is already tied to our bodies.
We find Habuba and Francis and fly
to the field by the road,
praying to Jesus that Jacob, the soldier,
is already there. We see him in silhouette
with the moon at his back.

My mother and Jacob talk in low voices.
I look at Habuba wrapped in white muslin
and remember we do not have the clothes
Habuba sewed, the cloths to wrap our heads
from the sun, the batik tops. I have only
the beads she threaded into my hair.
She looks at me, her eyes steady.
"You and your mother and Francis are going,"
she says. "I will come later."
"No, Habuba!" I cry out, my voice a harsh whisper. "No."
She remains still like a mountain. A moan builds inside me.
"I will let my hair grow and you will
plait me when I come," she says.
I press my hand to her hair.
It's cropped close to her head.
"You and Francis," I call to my mother.
"You go. I will come later with Habuba."
But my grandmother shoves me ahead.
"It is the duty of the children. That's why you must go.

I am not strong. I will hold you back."
Then she whispers, "You are my *mahbub*.
You are my favorite. Study. Bring us wealth. Go."

I begin to walk, following my mother
and Jacob and Francis
single file,
breathing in Habuba's scent of thyme.

# Shadows with Guns

We follow Jacob, silent, through the forest
away from Juba on the path he says is clear.
After ten minutes or fifteen, he says,
"Take the old paths through the jungle.
Two days or three.
Avoid the main roads. If you travel the main roads,
the SPLA soldiers will take you."
Jacob opens out his arm toward the dense
moonlit bush that would lead us south to Kenya.
"Only travel at night." He directs us ahead of him.
We see the shape of his stooped back.
Jacob turns to leave us deep in the bush.
I am terrified.
A step further, he stops and looks back.
"Lions, not so many," he calls. "But soldiers."
He lifts his arms as if they hold a weapon to blast.
We watch him. My body shakes. Francis lifts my hands
and drops his head to rest inside them.

Then an explosion nearly knocks us off the ground.
Mortar rounds!
They fly close by. I know the *shhhhhh* and the blast.
Then round after round after round
like rain.
Which way to run? My mother and Francis and I
pull in different directions, but we can't let go
of each other.

Jacob has disappeared. He has his coins.
Then silence.
Rebel soldiers could spring out from the bush
and accuse us of spying for the government.
They would take my mother and me for wives
and Francis to carry their guns.
Or government soldiers could see us cross back into Juba.
They, too—*Spies!* they will say—and bloody us to tell them
SPLA rebel secrets.
We must run. Where? I see shadows everywhere.
But we must run. Somewhere! This is not a place to hide.
"We have to go back," I shout. We hold on to each other
and to Francis. Finally we race across the path,
trying to retrace our steps by each cluster of stones.
I race. My only certainty—we cannot stop.
See! There are my little brother's running legs
and shining eyes.
Ahhh, my foot is only meters away
from the start of Jacob's path.
I am almost inside the city's prisonlike walls—
when I remember.
First comes the smell.
The stinking soldier's smell.
Then the sound
of his dark laughter as he turned to go.
He will return. That I know.
But we must retrace our footsteps
on the road in the dark
while clouds hide the moon.
Now every step inside Juba

is also a minefield,
laid by a soldier for me alone.
I know Habuba sees our shapes
slide into the dark courtyard.
His smell is still there.
Maybe he is outside in the dark—
simply waiting.
I fall in my grandmother's arms.
She does not ask.
"You are alive," is all she says.

# Flight

Every day my mother tries to contact Uncle Marko.
When she does, she shouts into the merchant's phone,
"Where is this priest who is friends with the UN?
It is time to call this priest. Did you forget you have family
in Juba? Other people are getting on the list.
But I do not see our name on the list. The government
soldiers at any time are coming door to door in the night.
Is that what you do in America, you forget you have family?"

We wait through the dry season, we wait till the rains begin.
Habuba does not talk about these plans with us.
She knows my chance of life in Juba
is as fragile as a single strand of hair.
At night I lie unsleeping
At night I lie with
the elephant bone
squeezed in my fist.

Maybe my mother wears down Uncle Marko
and the priest—wherever he is—
because one day we are on the list.
In a torrential rain, my mother, Francis, and I
leave Habuba again.
We climb in the belly of a UN plane,
families, households pressed together on its huge
silver floor. We rise over Juba, flying north toward Khartoum,

people screaming with hope, and fear, and nausea.
We rise above the Nile and trees heavy with fruit.
My mother holds my exhausted body to her bones.
This roar is our first sound of freedom.

# Khartoum to Us Is Thirst

When we disembark from the silver cargo plane,
we follow the stream of people to the camps
for the southern Sudanese,
far outside the city of Khartoum.
Here we know many who escaped the war.
On the way, an old auntie spreads her wares—bananas—
on the ground. They lie before her on a dirty burlap bag,
small bananas like a row of quarter moons.
We buy two bananas from the old auntie
to curb our appetites.
But then my throat becomes parched with thirst.
And I hear Francis say, "I need water."
"Do not think of it," my mother warns.
We can think of nothing else. Hunger and thirst.
When we see a mango tree heavy with fruit
beside a northern farmer's goats,
our feet can't stop themselves from running.
I steal some mangoes
and run away so fast, my lungs are burning.
My breath feels caught between inhaling
and exhaling. Can someone die from running?
But somehow my lungs expand,
and my breath reenters my body.
The mangoes only tease our thirsty throats.
"I need water," Francis says.
I, too, have never been so thirsty.
I forget my belly and my fear of

stubble-throated soldiers.
All my senses search for water.
When we see a herder's barrel,
we cannot resist the water.
We both drink until we feel relief.

In Juba, we had food. We had water.
Still, I am grateful to be alive on this new road.
Sometimes Francis rides on my back.
"I'm hungry, Keji. Keji, when will we have food?"
"Soon," I whisper. "Soon." I know the coins we've saved
are for the fare from Khartoum or, worse,
my mother might have to pay a soldier.

In the camp, people take us in.
They are hungry for news of Juba,
and we spend the evening sharing sorrowful tales.
You can lose yourself in these streets of plastic shelters,
but we stay only a few days. We have far to go.
They tell us to go to the Souq Arabi, a huge market
where there are buses traveling north.
The journey to the souq itself takes us all day.
At the bus station we stop by the vendors
and stuff our mouths with kisra and stew.
With our coins we buy bus fare
and wait from one day to the next for the
bus to come that will drive us north to Wadi Halfa.
Farther and farther from Habuba—
but closer and closer to freedom.

# Wadi Halfa, Northern Sudan

The bus is like a truck. We squat,
holding on to the side,
and even squatting, our bodies lean
into one another as we sleep.
We sleep all the hours it takes
to get to the next town.
At each town where the bus stops,
we wait for another bus, often waiting
for two or three days. I lose count
of the days it takes
to get to Wadi Halfa.

When we finally arrive in the most northern city
of Sudan, we ask fellow travelers,
"Where do we find the steamer to Aswan?"
As soon as we open our mouths in this city,
Wadi Halfa, each person knows we are from Juba.
Our language they find so funny.
We speak Arabi Juba, Juba Arabic.

My mother and I count our money,
haggle for tickets to board the steamer,
which they say will come in a week,
maybe, maybe not. Maybe two.
We wait.

On the day we finally depart,
Francis runs up and down the deck,

jumping between people who have gathered
and their bags. Peddlers carry their wares aboard,
plastic furniture, rolls of rugs, cooking pots, goats.
When Francis is exhausted from running,
he takes long naps. We are packed in among
a shopfull of baskets of every size and shape.
We find a good, big basket,
and this is where Francis sleeps
among the sea of people and their goods.

Still, with every shape that appears
between the tall baskets,
I remember the thin whiskery neck of the soldier,
and I wind tight like a snake beside my mother.

Francis has a full belly. He keeps popping up,
grinning, as we steam from Wadi Halfa
toward Aswan in Egypt, closer and closer
to the city where refugees go:
Cairo.

The hours fade one into another, and I unwind
slowly, feeling my body become the rhythm
of the boat.

"Wake up! Why do you sleep?" I call Francis
when the sun rises in a crimson haze
over the morning water.
"No," he murmurs, "my eyes are still sleeping."
When he does wake, he eats little of our bread and beans.
He can't seem to stay awake, even while the sun

beats down. In the night, we watch the sky.
The moon is golden and white and wobbly
like one of Habuba's wobbly round kisras
that I loved to eat.
"Let's play the moon game," Francis says.
"Can you tell the steamer to go to the moon?"
"This one goes to Egypt," I tease.
"The Moon Steamer is full."
We spend time making up ways
to touch the moon.
Even when he falls back asleep,
Francis makes my lips smile at our silliness.


But my brother cramps up in the night.
His body bends in half in agony.
At first he yells out,
but as the night lengthens,
he only sobs softly.
My mother offers him drops of water from the lid
of a baby bottle she uses for a cup.
I put my cheek to his,
feeling the power of the boat as it steams
through the water. I am surging toward Cairo.
But Francis seems like he is somewhere else.
His eyes sink deeper and deeper
into his head. He cannot eat. No one
has medicine. Other children around us sicken, too.
They soil themselves unstopping.
"Bad water," people say. Bad water in Wadi Halfa.

We glide past Abu Simbel, the Egyptian temple
where pharaohs guard the doorway.
I do not want to go on. I want to go back
to Habuba. She would give Francis clean water
and some herb to stop his cramps.


My mother holds Francis.
We huddle under blankets to ward off the cold air.
Maybe we are both thinking,
*What if we had continued on the road*
*south to Kenya?*
*Would Francis be healthy then?*
*Or would we all have died?*
My mother says, "We cannot know
if we could have gotten to Kenya,
and if we had, which would be worse, here or there?"
"I will take him for a while, Yumis," I say.
We cling together as the moon fades into fog.
My teeth begin to chatter. I try to clench my jaw,
but I cannot still my teeth.
"I'm cold," I tell my mother.
She clutches both me and Francis.
But it is a kind of cold she cannot warm.
It is coming from inside me
as I watch the cold fog take over the moon.
I do not say this either,
the thing I remember that Habuba told me:
*Death would do the calling.*
After we disembark at Aswan,

we take turns carrying Francis.
We are still miles from Cairo.
How many days do we wait at Aswan?
I hardly know, but every day
I carry Francis, and each day he feels lighter.
Finally, we board a train. My brother lies quiet.
I watch for the moon.
My mother is gone, getting us food
before the train departs. Francis sighs.
It is an old man's sigh.
"Maybe she will find some chicken," I say,
to entice him, knowing she never could.
He leans against me, and I wait
for each breath to rise and fall.
I will get him to America,
if his chest will only keep rising and falling,
I will find us a way to be free in America.
When our mother comes back in her red flip-flops,
a cloth tied around her thin waist,
she has bread and a small bowl of chicken stew!
"Eat," she says. "Eat."
The smell rouses Francis
and he opens his eyes and smiles.
We each pull off a piece of bread
and try to hold it and the chicken in our mouths,
but it is so rich and delicious, we gobble it.
Even Francis eats a bite.
My mother starts to sing the Jesus song
we used to sing while we worked.

*That's why I pray to you in the morning.*

*That's why I pray to you in the evening.*

I sing too,

*That's why I pray to you in the night time.*

*That's why I pray to you all the time.*

I sing into the night, hoping to shut out

the soldier who took my bride wealth

and seems to hold me with his bad luck.

Even now, I cannot seem to get away.

# Church of the Sudanese

In Cairo, people say,
go to the Church of the Sudanese.
This is where we carry Francis.
Since we left Khartoum, we have been traveling
or waiting to travel
for more than a month.
Dust circles us and covers our eyes,
clogging our throats and pressing our clothes
to our skin.
When we get to the church, a woman leads us inside
the courtyard, where the shadows
of trees sway on the wall.
Here Francis will have water and food
and I hope maybe medicine. She leads us
to a small room off the courtyard.
"Now you will have sweets," I whisper,
laying him on a mat. "I will make it up to you,
all the harm that has come on this journey."
The woman brings a cup of liquid. He barely sips.
I lie beside him. We are safe.
*I will bring you sweets.*
I go to sleep holding his hand.

In the morning,
it is my mother I see first.
She kneels beside us.
My brother is still.

His light weight is on my shoulder.
She lifts him from me,
cradles his lifeless body to her chest.
My mother opens her mouth, and a sound
comes—a long high cry
that fills my body.
I too feel like I weigh little except
for the weight of her cry,
and I lift myself from the mat.
I curl my body into my mother and brother
so that I can breathe.

Another woman's voice makes a shrill harmony.
Soon cries come from many corners of the church,
a high-pitched animal trilling, calling to Francis.
The voices wash over me. Someone's gentle hands
rest my head against her chest
as she sings.

Somehow the sun sets as it always does.
My mother and I sit in the garden
of the Church of the Sacred Heart, the real name
of the Church of the Sudanese.
We sit back-to-back, holding each other upright.
I can feel her bones and heartbeat.
The family beside us drinks sweet milk
they bought from the vendor, and its smell
mixes with the smell of jasmine and urine.
The smell makes me believe I won't want to eat again.
Eating seems like something I did when I was young.

I imagine Francis will come at any time.
I see his eager grin—how happy he was when
he found me after he thought that I was lost.
I knew anyone could die.
But not Francis.

# United Nations High Commissioner for Refugees

My mother and I sleep on a mat beneath mosquito netting
next to a blue plaster wall like the blue of Lake Nasser.
"Mother," I call in the morning when I wake up.
My mother does not answer.
I rise and dress in my broken sandals,
my skirt and T-shirt. "I can't sleep," I whisper.
"I can't lie here. I am going." She does not answer.
But she does not stop me. "Please," I say.
I lay my face against hers.

I step into the courtyard.
A boy my age, maybe older,
looks up from a tattered book.
"I'm sorry about your brother,"
the boy says to me.
I lower my head.
"I am Lokolumbe," he says.
"I'm Viola," I say.
Then I ask him if he knows
where people go to get refugee status.
"Of course," he says, "that is why we are all here."
After he gives directions,
I return to my mother.
"We must go to the office of the
United Nations High Commissioner for Refugees.

That is what the boy Lokolumbe said."
Still she does not answer.
*Where are you, Francis?* I want to say out loud.
*Come with me.*
I tie a blue scarf over my broken-off, undressed hair.
I think briefly of the red beads
Habuba tied into it. Was that the same hair?
What does hair matter when my mother
will not rise? I leave her alone,
but I leave her with our own women
and children in these rooms for the southern Sudanese.


I step into the orange haze of Cairo
and the Muslim call to prayer
and search for the office of the United Nations
High Commissioner for Refugees.
The air in the street is foul
and hazy from car exhaust. Here, the pathways
are made of stone, not the dust of Juba,
but they leave their own kind of grit.
Smells bite my nose.
Beside the stone path are bins of yellow powder
and fat peppers, and further on, bottles of sweet oils
and like a stab, I smell my grandmother's thyme oil.
Horns blast. A man calls out.
I forget the directions the boy gave me,
never imagining a city could be this alive at dawn.
Ladies dressed all in white to the tops of their heads
walk in high heels, as tall as ostriches.
I feel something wet hit my face.

The wet falls over my eyelids.
"*Abeed*"—slave—a man yells. "Go home."
I lunge at him as he laughs. I would take out his eyes
if I could catch him. "I am not a slave!"
I scrub his spit with my scarf.

Fiat, Jeep, Nissan, Toyota, Mitsubishi,
I focus on the cars and stop looking at the people.
I try to remember the names of all the cars.
*Francis, you would love to see these cars.*
*Francis, you would race between them, shrieking!*

# Waiting to Become a Refugee

I see a line of people just as Lokolumbe has told me,
Only the line is fifty and more people long.
"We have come too late," a girl tells me.
"Tomorrow I will come at five o'clock."
"In the morning?" I ask.
"Yes, then maybe I can talk to someone."

The next morning, I wake at 4:00 a.m.
"Mother," I call, "we must go
to the United Nations High Commissioner for Refugees."
"Not now," she answers.
She will sleep another day.
Once again I go alone, speaking to Francis in my mind.
This time I do not get lost. I am in line by five o'clock.
But I do not get in.
For many mornings, this is my job. I wake
to meet the orange haze and the million cars.

Then one morning, my mother rises.
She covers her head with a red scarf and walks
onto the street. I don't know where she could be going.
I follow. I see her red scarf ahead of me, and I follow
through the streets of mud brick houses on the edge
of the desert. She does not have a destination,
I think. Does she think Francis is only lost
and she might find him?

When I catch up, I explain the things I
hear people say in the streets.
"8,000 of us are waiting in Cairo,
Sudanese, Somalis, Yemenis, Sierra Leoneans,
all waiting for our refugee status.
We all want America, especially Lokolumbe.
He knows most of the states and their capital cities
so that he'll be ready for any state they pick for him."

My mother listens to my words, but she cannot take in
the enormity. She focuses on Lokolumbe.
"I know this boy's mother. They are from Juba."

# No Elephants Here

After many weeks, I bring an application home
from the High Commissioner for Refugees.
My mother and I fill in the words we know.
They say, we will call you for the interview.
They never call.
Lokolumbe says, "Three times they promised me
an interview and they never interviewed me."
Lokolumbe has been here three years. Waiting.
I lie in bed that night and do not sleep.

But maybe I do sleep because in the dawn
I am suddenly aware of wind.
I wake and wonder, Am I in my bed in Juba?
I will fetch water, and Habuba will boil the water.
Then I hear the breath of sleeping mothers
and children. I smell Cairo, the Cairo that does not sleep.
I open my eyes. In the dim light I see children's tiny
shirts hung on a palm tree to dry. The shape of them
makes me remember Francis's shoulders
the day the soldier said, "Come."
I was terrified for him.
I wanted to save him.
I could not save him.
I sit up, and something hard drops to the floor.
The book Habuba gave me.
I clutch it to my belly.
Habuba.

I hold it to me and breathe
as if I could breathe life back into us all.


In the street,
I drop my head back and let the wind
cool my skin.
Just as I have done on hot nights
in our courtyard in Juba,
I shut my eyes.
In that second, the smell hits me like a fist.
The sweet molasses smell of tobacco.
My eyes flash open
and I see a group of Egyptian
men cross the street,
coming toward me.
I run.
Francis is not here.
I do not have to protect Francis,
and so I run barefoot down the stone path the way
I could not have run from the soldier.
The men do not race in my footsteps,
but I keep running from the memory of the soldier.
Sweat drops from my eyes and my cheeks,
even in the rain.
His single word, "Come," blasts in my ears.
I race.
But he is always there on the sweet tobacco smell.
When I stop, I will feel his hand.
*Come.*
*NO!*

Nausea stops me far from my mother.
I squat in the windy dark and I retch.
I feel his hard palm again across my lips
and then the fist. I feel my body tear open again.
There is no running fast enough
or quinine bitter enough
to stop the remembering.
There are no elephants here.
I can't even find one in my dreams.

# Minutes

In the morning, my mother rises before I do.
I see her shoulder against the blue stucco wall.
"Yumis?" I call. *Mommy?*
"We must get jobs," she answers, reaching for a cloth
and covering herself so that only her red flip-flops show.
"I have heard of cleaning jobs in the rich area," she says.
Not till I hear the strength in her voice do I know
how much I've missed my mother.
If my mother is here,
maybe I am here, too.

In the orange haze,
she buys sweet milk from the vendor.
We drink among groups of families,
our shoulders touching.
I am hungry, and we drink from the same cup
and split an orange,
and both of us are sticky with the juice.

My mother borrows a cell phone with *minutes*—
we learn this word. With a job you can buy *minutes*.
She vows she is getting a job and will pay this person back.
In the church courtyard, her back rounds over the phone,
and she pushes the numbers that Marko had sent to us.
Then she shouts into the phone, "Ey, Marko, is this you?
We are now coming to America. Please give us the
information.

What is happening in Juba? Where is everyone?
What is happening?" She barrages him with questions
and cannot stop to listen. Finally she commands,
"You talk to Keji." I press the phone to my ear.
"No, we are not coming now," I say.
"We are waiting for an interview."
I listen. This uncle I do not remember
tells me important numbers to put on the paper.
But then the phone dies. I sit with my mother.
"He says maybe he can talk to Habuba on some phone."
My mother makes a grunting sound. I think it is a shock,
our new life. How did this happen?
All of us away from each other. All of us eating alone.
Only connected by minutes.

# Tall Girl Wants Job

Sudanese girls my age get jobs here. I know this.
I would never have a job in Juba, but here, there are
lowly, illegal jobs for the southern Sudanese.
Maybe someone in this haze of people
will hire a tall girl who has kept house
since she was the age of five.

In the morning, my mother and I pass Bedouin people
stitching bright-colored
blossoms and spirals of leaves on fabric.
We pass barrels of peppers and seeds and beans.
We pass the clicking of dominoes.
We walk in the growing heat to the east side of the Nile.
Felucca boats glide on the river, nothing
like the churning steamer we traveled on.
Juba is on the Nile River, too, but at home, the Nile
has beds of rocks and sometimes a hippopotamus.
That is where my mother once found the elephant bone.
Our eyes follow the tall lines of buildings that reach
the sky. Cars shoot past the river on six roads side by side.
It is along this road that we find the rich area.
We look for jobs in a building with towers
called the Cairo World Trade Center.
In these tall towers, after many, many weeks,
we both get jobs cleaning.
Here, I will earn clean coins.

Every week I put these coins
into our soft pouch. On Sundays,
in the hour when the sun drops,
we count it. With the money, we can buy
the vendor's bread to give us strength to walk.
And we can save for America.
I cannot imagine my future,
and my past is a snake always ready
to strike.

# Sahara

We know our tribe in Cairo
by the way we move,
us southern Sudanese.
Lokolumbe is a Bari.
He becomes my tall brother.
"Where do you want to go in America?" I say.
We are practicing English.
"Bismarck," he says, "Bismarck, North Dakota.
That is the best place. *Sweet*," he adds,
a new way to use *sweet*, which I like.
"Where do you want to go?" he asks.
I have a vague memory of the rhythm
I heard on the road in Juba
and see the boy with the glistening back.
*Be free.*
But now I say,
"I don't know.
I don't belong anywhere anymore."
I tell Lokolumbe,
"I no longer braid my hair since it is broken.
I used to braid girls' hair in our courtyard in Juba.
I used to give my cousin little twists with bright beads.
We are all separated now, those children and me."
I tell him I see girls on Cairo streets who braid extensions
into their own hair to make it longer or thicker.
But I don't touch my hair.
I don't tell him how it hurts, remembering
the feel of Habuba's fingers braiding my hair.

Instead I say, "I am not who I used to be.
We were three, like three strands.
We lay, three of us, on the steamer, warming each other.
Without the third, I don't know what to do."


Lokolumbe tells me two stories.
We are walking beyond the gold domes and resorts
on the sand of the Sahara. If I keep walking
forever, I could return to Sudan.
Here is his first story.
It is many boys' story.
"I was conscripted by the northern army.
They wanted to send me to the south
to kill our people. But I fled to the camps
near Khartoum. All of my family is dead."
I think this is why, when he talks,
he talks only about America.


I like the second story.
"They say if you see only the desert
day after day
and nothing but sand is in your view,
you can see forever into your own mind."


As days stretch into months,
Lokolumbe and I begin to walk the desert.
It is true. Since there is nothing but sand,
I peer deep into my mind.
I see my fingers riding my mother's
fingers when I learned to braid.

I ask Lokolumbe,
"What does it matter about a refugee's hair?
Why not have knots like a child? What does it matter?"
He looks ahead into the sand.
As tall as I am,
I come only to Lokolumbe's shoulder.
He does not answer at first.
We both keep walking in the desert,
following a fragile dream of America.
"Braids are from our culture," he says, this boy who reads
and knows all the American capital cities.
"They are the African designs we give to the world.
When you are ready, you will braid."

# Viola and Lokolumbe English Night School

We go back to the church and here
Lokolumbe brings his book. It is a fat book
with the name *Responding to Literature.*
I get my book. "What do you have?" he asks.
I show him Habuba's hymnal in Bari.
Few can read Bari,
and we recruit a translator.
Lokolumbe pulls out papers from his pockets.
Word by word, an old auntie translates one hymn
from Bari into Arabic. I translate the Arabic
into English. With a pencil I write tiny words
in English over the Bari
in the flimsy pages of the hymnal.
I ask Lokolumbe, "Do you have any other book
you are not reading?" He says yes, he does.
Lokolumbe had moved to a room with many boys
in the Arba'a wa Nuss section of Cairo.
He says the next time he comes from there,
he will bring a new book. And he does.
He brings many books, all books from the West,
especially America. He brings mystery stories,
such as one by Walter Mosley. These are good.
From these books I learn about clothes styles
and boyfriends and dangerous jobs in America.
We also both like to read *Responding to Literature,*

full of poems and stories. We have the idea
to *establish*—Lokolumbe's word—
The Viola and Lokolumbe English Night School.
In our school, we read *Responding to Literature*
out loud. It has 1,218 pages. We are on page 16,
"Theme for English B" by Langston Hughes.


One day missionaries come with an English book called
*Just So Stories*. I read to Lokolumbe the story of
how a baby elephant got his trunk.
We laugh so hard in that sun-drenched courtyard
over words like *blotchy, stripy, speckly, slippery-slidy*.
I wonder if Habuba would be proud of my school teaching.
Over the months, we read all the *Just So Stories*,
the *Daily Standard*, the *USA Today*, hymns
from 1—"New Every Morning Is the Love"—through
299—"Let Saints on Earth in Concert Sing."
and *Responding to Literature* up to page 952,
"There Was a Child Went Forth" by Walt Whitman.
It makes me think of Francis
and all he could have been
if he went forth.
Maybe if I were a teacher—a most respected person—
I could bring honor to my small brother
and all the things he might have done
when he became a man.


The Viola and Lokolumbe English Night School
meets every night for nearly two years.

My mother and I go to the High Commissioner for Refugees
when they call for more interviews.
My mother shouts at them, "Why do you keep asking us?
We have told all the stories about our lives that we know."
In the night we sleep in the courtyard of the Church
of the Sudanese with other mothers and children.
I turn sixteen and seventeen years old here.
Lokolumbe has become my tall older brother.
What will I do if he leaves for Bismarck, North Dakota?

# Blue Card

On the edge of the hottest desert season,
I drag my tired body home from fourteen hours
of cleaning. Here I see a circle of people,
hear voices high with excitement.
And inside the circle is my mother.
She reaches her arm out to me through the crowd.
In her hand is a small vinyl case. I have seen vendors
sell cases like this. I study her face.
"What is this?" I say.
Inside I see it. The blue card that means
we are eligible for resettlement. I catch my breath.
"We are going?"
"Yes, we go."
My mother is smiling.
I see her mouth and her squeezed-up eyes smiling.
Is this woman my mother? This woman—smiling!
"Francis, we are going!" I jump, my arms in the air.
But I keep looking at my mother's smile—
it's as if I am just seeing her now.
I know it is only because of her that I am still alive.
It is as if we breathe the same breath. When she puts
aseeda in her mouth, I feel like I have eaten.
She did not send me away from her in Juba.
I touch her smiling lips. She is myself.

My mother is already instructing me:
"We will prepare food for a party with our neighbors.

They have been very, very good to us."
The crowd hums throughout the courtyard.
The party will be big.
Some of these people are going to America, too.
Then my eyes find Lokolumbe.
Did he get a blue card? I see from his eyes
that he did not. He will not go to Bismarck,
Saint Paul, Atlanta, Boston.
His shoulders sag, but then he straightens his back.
Is he remembering the vastness
of the desert?
"Where are you going?" he asks.
My mother shows him the paper.
Portland, Maine, U.S.A.
He raises his head in proud recognition.
"Augusta," he says. "The capital of Maine is Augusta."

# Lokolumbe

Lokolumbe and I exchange addresses.
I write mine in *Responding to Literature*.
He writes his in Habuba's hymnal.
His address is the Church of the Sudanese,
because wherever he goes, he will know people there.
Mine is my uncle's address
with a street name and a zip code.
"You will come soon," I say.
We walk into the desert, where we walked
many times. "Yes," he says. "Very soon."
If they never interview him and close his case,
I know he will still say, "Yes, very soon."
Cairo is the place I leave both him
and my little brother.
"Who will you read with?" I ask.
"I don't know."
"I will send you a book," I say.
"I would like Walter Mosley," he says.
"My heart hurts," I say.
"Yes, our hearts hurt," he says.
He strides ahead of me in the sand and wind.
He turns. "Only African girls can do the braids."

# Part Two
# *Elephant Footsteps*

Portland, Maine
United States
2002–2003

# White

All these people in the Portland airport are white!
They are light-skinned people like many northern
Sudanese who cause us so much sorrow.
I knew they would not be African like me,
but they are all so white!
Flashes of light break open the sky here.
Rain is falling! I missed rain in Cairo.
A very big man—definitely not white—
comes toward us. He shakes my mother's hand
and my hand, and suddenly when he talks,
I see the bright of Habuba's eyes in his.
This is Marko!
He must be brave to come to the airport
while the sky is breaking apart.
In Cairo, it did not rain. I remember only days of heat
and the winds blowing across the desert.
It's been so long since I tasted Juba rain.
Under a flashing sky, Marko drives us to the place
where we will live. I am so cold. I wear a sweatshirt
with a hood the UN people gave me when we left Egypt,
but it is not enough to keep me warm.
The UN also gave us our tickets,
and Marko says people here in Portland collected
furniture and food for us. At the place where we'll live,
people from Catholic Charities show us three rooms,
and I wonder if they live here, too.
One whole room they say is for my mother. It has a bed

the size for a queen, say the welcome people.
They also bring a jar of mashed peanuts, sliced meat,
a television—something that would make Habuba's
eyes pop—shiny, sweet fruits whose skin you can eat,
and Hershey's Bars.
My mother raises her arms in the air then,
brings her palms together at her chest,
crying out in delight.
"We are most grateful," she whispers.
Her arms rise once more. "Most grateful."
What would Francis love the most?
I ask for a chocolate bar.
I remember the mangoes we stole from the farmer
and the emptiness of our bellies. How we ate mangoes
for days when traveling north. How Francis grinned
when he bit into one.
"This bed is for you," the people say to me
about a second bed in a separate bedroom.
It is a good bed even if, when I try it,
my feet fall off the end.
But then they leave, the white people and my uncle.
My mother and I are alone in rooms that flow
one to another, far from the Cairo courtyard
where we rested among dozens of sleeping families.
Exhausted, my mother and I lie down on the queen bed,
our legs outstretched,
one of my legs crossed over hers like logs
on the Nile.
But tight as we are, a hole remains

where Francis is supposed to be.
I drop into sleep and see him.
He smells like chocolate in my dream.
But when I awake, it's my own skin I am smelling.

# America

Marko brings us to a store—the biggest store in the world,
Walmart. Nothing like the souq with barrels of spices,
cardamom, curry powders, mustard seeds, and nutmeg.
"Spices are here," Marko says, but they are in small
tins and bottles. We have a card to buy food.
We walk up and down the rows. Marko and his daughter,
my cousin Jackie, tell us the names of everything:
blueberries, sponge cake, squeaking toys for dogs.
Marko shows us how to buy a phone card that gives us
minutes to talk to people in Sudan and Cairo.
Marko also puts two cell phones in our shopping basket.
"In America,"
he says, "everyone has."

At home, my mother hangs photos of my father and Francis.
I have not thought of my father,
but seeing him on the wall,
I realize my mother must think of him all the time.
With my mother's cell phone and the phone card,
we try to call a Juba number Marko says
sometimes goes through. We get only static.
I want to tell Habuba we have two beds.
I want to tell her about blueberries
and sponge cake. I want to cook with her
and let our voices dance and circle
while we work. That is the normal way.
My mother is busy with the people at Catholic Charities.

When she comes home, she says we have to find jobs
so we can pay for rent and heat and electricity,
things we had no need for in Sudan.
How do we get so much money?

In our kitchen, we have a long loaf of crusty bread
and sharp cheese, and now we have a bag of sugar.
We add spoonfuls of sugar to our tea.
I remember a time in Sudan when people went for days
filling their bellies with water lilies.

Jackie's mom, my aunt Rita, complains to my mother,
"The hard thing is English.
They cannot understand our perfectly good English.
They think we are speaking some other tongue.
If they would just listen. If you do not talk like them,
they say you are ignorant.
When they talk to you they are yelling.
We have to educate these people. We have to say,
*We have been to school.* Maybe not like your school.
Maybe we did not have so many pens and papers.
But we are *not* ignorant." My mother listens
and pushes buttons on her new telephone,
calling families in Portland we once knew in Juba.
Marko goes to work, and Jackie goes to a job in the mall,
a place with more stores, she says, than I have ever seen.
When they are gone, it is just my mother and me,
and no one else seems to be in these rows
of wooden buildings called apartments.
Where is everybody?

# Kennedy Park

In the evening, when some people have come home,
Jackie and I sit on the concrete steps
outside our apartment.
Jackie wears a short skirt and strapless top.
This girl is brave. We would die
if we dressed this way in Juba.
I wear the jeans and sweatshirt
the UN people gave me.
A neighbor man passes and does not stare,
does not seem shocked
at Jackie's bare legs.
My mother and I have slept three nights in our bed.
It is after 7 o'clock,
and the sun still shines.
"It is light here most of the time," I say.
"Not always," Jackie says.
Jackie lives in another apartment
in these streets of wooden buildings.
She and my uncle and aunt escaped years before us.
"The dark doesn't come till very late," I say.
"It's summer," she says. "The days are long.
In the winter it gets dark sooner.
Short days and long days.
That's what they have here."
Jackie is taking the braided hair extensions
from her hair so her head can breathe.
We do this—letting our heads breathe—in Juba.
I say, "At home,

we'd have to get the paraffin for the lamp
at this time of the day if the electricity cut off."
"Do you think I don't remember?" Jackie says.
"If you live in Kennedy Park, you remember.
The elders make sure you remember.
Your mother makes sure you remember.
If you go to McDonald's, your mother makes you remember,
'You need African food,' she says.
'*You* cannot eat this food. You will die!'
That's what they say if you forget to remember."


I do not help Jackie to release the bands
that lock her extensions as I would have done
so naturally for any girl in Juba.
I watch the sun go down.
Jackie and other teenagers stay on the lawn
and talk. Two boys shoot baskets.
Cars pull between yellow parking lines
painted on new tar. America smells like tar
and damp and salty air.
Asian girls in sleek skirts
run down the sidewalk to a waiting car.
Some boys have *djembes*, and the drumbeat
warms our talk. "You want me to braid extensions
in your hair?" Jackie asks.
"Let it grow a little. I'll do that for you."
I shake my head.
Jackie talks about going on a car trip
to a place called Manchester,
where they sell extensions and oils
for African hair.

Jackie talks while her fingers fly
through her braids. "I don't like how people here
think we are from the jungle,"
she says. "But I am not hungry here.
I am not afraid. Soldiers don't
break down our door."
My mind flashes
through images as she talks.
*My grandmother dabs the scent of thyme on my arm.*
*Our rations are tied under my dress.*
*They dig into my ribs.*
*The soldier lunges.*
*Dirt fills my nostrils.*
*I gasp for breath.*

"You're on Juba time. Gonna take a while."
I swallow. "Yes."
I bring my mind back to this place—Kennedy Park,
the basketball hammering on blacktop,
the pause
when they shoot.
In Juba, it's seven hours later,
it's early morning,
and terror spills like hot oil
onto my limbs.

"Where is the school?" I ask.
She laughs. "This is summer vacation. No school."
No school?
Lokolumbe and I always had school.

In our bathroom, along with a flushing toilet
and an indoor shower *and* a sink,
we have something else that is rare in Juba:
a mirror as wide as a girl.
That night I stand at the mirror
and see my ragged, broken hair.
With scissors I cut, cut,
cut, until my hair all around
is cut as close to my head as I can make it.
When I am done,
I gaze at my unflinching eyes.
*Hey*! I tell Lokolumbe,
*this is the way I look in America.*

# Miss America Abby

Abby comes. She is my American mentor
assigned to me by Catholic Charities.
She says, "Think of me like a big sister."
Her hair is wavy like a curving flower.
Pale brown with strands of red.
She sits on our new couch and crosses her
bare legs. I have Miss America for my mentor!
She has good teeth, which would make her a
valuable bride. When she talks, beads
the color of blueberries dance
between strands of her hair.
She says I can walk to my school.
"But if you want to be cool, don't."
We get in her car—her boyfriend's, she says—
so she can show the school to me. She tells me,
"Buckle your seat belt."
"I don't like it," I say.
"Well you have to, or the police will get you."
"Why do the police care if I buckle my seat belt?"
"So you don't die in an accident," she says.
This is stunning to me. Why would police,
who to me are like soldiers, even notice if I die?
Abby drives up in front of a building
larger than any building in Juba.
It is as large or more than the Church
of the Sudanese in Cairo. It has arches.
I lift my chin and stretch my neck to see.

Above the arches are stone carvings.
To enter the door, you must climb a staircase.
Carved in the stone are the words, "Portland High School."
"Pretty old," Abby says. "I went here.
My mom went here. My gran went here.
My whole family went here after they came
from Ireland. Come on, I'll show you."
"This is a school?" is all I can say.
My school in Juba had a few large rooms with cracked
plaster walls. My room had a blackboard
and 50 seats where we sat two by two.
Once more, my eyes follow the stairs
to the wide door.
"You must have studied English," she says.
"School was in Arabic," I say.
"When I was young, they burned our English books."
"Who did?" she says.
"The soldiers. They put you in jail for using English.
It's still inside me, the English."
Beside Miss America Abby, I climb the stairs.
"Sweeeet," I say. I lift my arms high like
Habuba would if she could imagine
a school as big as a church.
Abby laughs at my *sweeeet*.
"We practiced English in Cairo—
my friend Lokolumbe and me—
for when we came to America."
Abby lists off all the supplies
she says a girl needs in high school.
"You'll have English here, too, and math,

U.S. history, a science class,
all with a bunch of other kids in ESL."
I sigh.
I think of the one book I have—
Habuba's hymnal
in Bari, Arabic, and English.
I look up at the school reaching into the sky
with grand clouds floating by
and I burst out laughing.
Or maybe I am crying.
Am I really here?
The world is upside down.

# Dish

My mother gets a job at a chicken packing company.
With one of her first paychecks, she buys a
satellite dish so we can hear news from Sudan.
My uncle bolts it to a railing outside our door.
Soon many Sudanese begin to gather
at our house because we have a dish.
We get daytime programs Jackie calls the soaps.
They are in Arabic from Cairo.
Then we watch the war in Sudan on Al Jazeera's news.
Uncle Marko comes by to watch.
Aunt Rita and Jackie come, too.
And Frieda, my mother's friend,
with her little boy, Jamal, who wears
tiny green slippers and is learning to do somersaults.
Lado, who works in the African restaurant,
drops by, and so does Miss America Abby.
People gather in the living room, draping
on our long American couch and sitting around
the glass coffee table after eating chicken and stew.
Jackie and I wash and wipe the dinner pots.
Jamal runs in and out between the rows of beads
we hung in the doorway to the back hall.
Charles, a Sudanese neighbor, enters,
shakes everyone's hands as each visitor has done,
and drops into our one armchair.
He smells of the grease of the car shop where he works.
Why does Charles come?

He already has two wives, Kadat in Kennedy Park
and a new one in Riverside. Jackie widens her eyes
at me in the kitchen and whispers,
"Don't his wives cook for him?"
But already my mother, bone by bone,
lifts herself from the couch
and cooks more chicken for him.
A woman must do this. My mother
does not need to even wave her hand at me.
I know I must serve him the food.
Jackie is shaking her head at Charles. And I think
I don't want my mother to be wife number three.
I want to tell him, I'll be a teacher. I'll bring her wealth.
When I'm slow to bring Charles a plate,
my mother's tongue turns sharp.
"Keji, ungrateful girl. You will treat him
as you learned to treat a man in Africa.
Did you think you survived to come here
and show such disrespect?"
When the chicken is done, I get him a plate.
But I do not bring him tea.
Charles watches the large TV screen. He says,
"Viola, you are too old to go to school.
You should prepare chickens like your mother."
My mother may not care if I go to school.
But if I want to become educated, I know better
than to argue with this man.
Next time I will bring him tea.

# Cell Phones

Suddenly all the room is silent.
John Garang's wide Dinka face fills the screen.
My mother stretches her arm toward the TV
and clicks up the volume on the remote.
Abby is about to lecture my mother about school.
I tell her, "Wait."
Dr. John is the rebel leader of the southern Sudanese.
John Garang commands that we must keep Sudan united,
the south with the north. We click our tongues.
We trust him like a two-edged blade.
The newsman announces,
"Twenty-seven people were killed in fighting
near the government stronghold of Juba."
Instantly guests dial the 100-number on their
African Dream calling cards, they dial the PIN,
they dial the country code.
They are fast, my American relatives,
pressing cell phones to their ears.
Lado presses two, one to each ear,
one to Khartoum, even though it is 4 a.m. there,
one to Ohio, where more relatives live.
They phone relatives in Cairo and Nairobi.
"What is happening in Juba?" they are all asking.
We learn about one family we know well
who have arranged to call friends in Cairo. In the chaos
I say, "How can we talk to Habuba?"
Maybe we can, if we find someone who will allow us

to use their connection—maybe a merchant—
and beg them to go and find her and keep her there
until the time we try to connect from America.
And even then it might not work.
Someone in Minneapolis says it was a minefield,
and nineteen rebels died. Someone in Cairo
says no, it was civilians fleeing to Juba from
a village under rocket attack. No one knows
which village. No one knows anything,
but the phones keep ringing. My phone,
the second one Marko bought for us at Walmart,
has no minutes. It won't have minutes
until I get a job, but I pretend. I hold it to my ear.
"Habuba," I whisper.
I sit on a chair beside my mother, my arm over my head.
"Habuba," I say again. I squeeze my eyes shut.
All the journey disappears.
Portland to New York: 234 miles,
New York to Cairo: 5,621 miles,
Cairo to Juba: 1,730 miles.
Lokolumbe and I mapped these in school.
I pretend to tell her, "I'll call you,
Habuba. I'll get an African Dream card."
In my mind she says, *Insha'Allah*—God willing.
I describe my school to her.
She is impressed.
Then I am sucked into that night,
the smell of thyme on my body.
I think of the scorching trek to the camp
of people of the south near Khartoum.

What if Habuba had tried to come with us?
Could she have made that journey?

There are a million chinks
along the miles to stop
the miracle of her voice in my ear
here in America.
A million places that can break down and fail.
I promise I will keep trying to call her.
I imagine Habuba holding my mother's phone card,
turning the card in her palm.
This is what she would see:
two elephants, facing trunk to trunk,
under a burst of African sun.

# My Teacher

My mother has decided.
I will clean the house,
I will get a job.
I will buy the food and cook.
This is the way for African daughters.
They take care of the house.
Habuba would say so, too,
but she will be very glad that my mother
does not keep me from school
so long as the meals are prepared.

School! I am overjoyed.

On the first day of school,
Jackie and I climb the stone stairs and enter
a kingdom with globes of light above our heads
and painted tiles on the walls. I think I have
gone to the Jesus heaven.

I sit in my school in Mrs. Mejía's ESL class.
Mrs. Mejía is very old with hair too black for her age
and bright red lipstick.
She is almost as tall as me.
"Study and you will be queen of the world,"
she says, leaning low. I can see her chest.
Then she is up, her arms open wide.
"Study and you will be rich."

No one in Sudan has lived as long as Mrs. Mejía,
who paints her fingernails the color of red peppers.
Mrs. Mejía gives me three things the first day:
a pen, a paperback English dictionary, and a poem.

Mrs. Mejía wears makeup
like the stars in the Egyptian soaps.
Mrs. Mejía is from a country called Colombia.
No one in America is from America.

# Library

Mrs. Mejía takes my ESL class to the library.
We gather around her. I am the tallest and can see over
the head scarf of a Somali girl. Mrs. Mejía tells us to find
a book of poems, check it out, and take it home.
I worry about the poems. How can I afford them?
She opens a small book.
With one arm in the air
and her red fingernails dancing,
she reads a poem called
"Spring-Watching Pavilion."
I don't completely understand it,
though I like the way it sounds.
It opens with the lines

> *"A gentle spring evening arrives*
> *airily, unclouded by worldly dust."*

And ends with:

> *"Where is nirvana?*
> *Nirvana is here, nine times out of ten."*

I'd like to discuss nirvana with Lokolumbe tonight.

When Mrs. Mejía says again that we should each
pick a book, one student says she forgot her money.
"This is not a *librería*, a bookstore. You don't have to pay.
These are books you borrow. When you find your book,
take it to the desk and show your student ID."
My eyes follow a red, gold, and blue river of books
up one shelf, then circling to the next shelf and the next.
I can take any of these? Habuba, you cannot imagine.

# Water

A red-haired boy is in my Foods A–Z class.
I call it cooking, something I know how to do well.
It is less hard for me than English and history.
The boy is going to be a seafood chef.
He tells me this with flour up to his elbows and
streaks on his nose. I have never seen a boy cook before.
He takes a boat with his father to the big, blue bay.
He says I could come, too. That night,
I cook for my mother, and we talk about the sea.
We talk while she lies on the couch with her elbow
over her head beneath the photos of my father and Francis.
Her eyes are sad. She does not sleep well.
She snaps at me often: "Keji, sweep the floor."
"Keji, scrub the bathroom." I am used to her temper,
but now when she shouts, my chest tightens;
a pain shoots through me. I think malaria would be better
than what is happening to my heart in this apartment
with only my mother and me.
But tonight we are talking about water.
I tell her I don't like the water here. I don't tell her
about the red-haired boy who fishes in the bay.
My mother and I remember the Nile.
The Nile is wide and warm
and smells like carrots or clean fruit.
Here the water smells strong like fish and salty monsters
people catch from the ocean floor.
"In Sudan before the war," my mother tells me,
"people from Juba ate small fish

with silver scales and white flesh.
Your grandfather caught them from a long riverboat
with a mast and boom cut from trees.
In the dry season, he set up a cattle camp on an island
in the Nile where grazing was good."
She said Habuba told stories
about piling into dugouts with her cousins,
going to see their beloved cattle.
Remembering the Nile takes
some of the sadness from her eyes.
"Did Habuba ever tell you," I say,
"Who follows the elephant will have no problems?"
When I see a small smile come on her lips,
I know she had.

# The Cemetery

Miss America Abby says come walk with her
and her spotted dog, Elsa.
We do, and the moon shows in the daylight sky.
The wind whips her hair with its golden streaks.
In this place are stones, and Abby says
people are buried here under the ground.
Since I know more people
who have died than are alive, I like it here.
Trees fill the sky with gold and orange leaves.
Other tall, straight trees have needles that swirl
to the ground and make a fragrant bed I walk on.
Abby has a camera and photographs the stones and leaves
that spiral through the wind.
"I'd like to photograph you," she says. "In all these leaves.
You should send some photos to a modeling agency.
You'd be perfect." I can't pay attention to her camera.
I am wandering here with the dead people I remember.
Soon the wind grows so strong, it's hard for us to stand.
We hear a thunderous crash beyond us through the trees.
In that instant I'm back in Juba, surrounded by gunfire.
I drop to the ground.
Abby takes my hand and tugs me. "Look," she says,
"It's that tree."
I rise, and we run.
I see a tree that has crashed on its belly in our path,
and I reach up to the gnarled trunk where it rests
on the tops of its branches.

The trunk is as high as my shoulder
and as massive as an elephant.
I can smell the skin and the gold and orange leaves
on limbs severed from its trunk.
Suddenly it is a breathing animal to me.
It *is* an elephant. I touch its bark and belly.
Inside, the new pale tree is alive. Its leaves quiver,
its elephant body is thick and rough.
I stretch my arm over the body and rest my head.
The sky is now cloudless blue.
I feel powerful.
I made a tree into an elephant.

# Why I Don't Have Braids

Many Sudanese girls live in Kennedy Park.
Sometimes Jackie and I hang out with them
and listen to a Congolese band on the TV.
One girl is Poni, another girl from Juba
who might have even played with me
in our courtyard when we were little.
Poni is a rebel; she would like to be a girl SPLA
with her proclamations:
*South Sudan all day every day till the day I die.*
Jackie braids extensions into the tender hair
around Poni's temple,
then in a line across her crown.
I close my eyes.
I feel Habuba's fingers when she made lines of braids
in my hair.
I think of Lokolumbe when we walked in the desert,
my head covered with a shawl,
my hair untended. "Here," Lokolumbe had said,
"you can see deep into your mind."
And I could. I saw the missing strands of my family.
And the bride wealth missing from myself.
I thought I would have a better chance in America
than in the camps in Kenya, but here in America
I must hold these desert places all by myself.
Sometimes I miss Lokolumbe more than anyone.
And still I haven't tried to call him.
I have not sent him books by his favorite author,

Walter Mosley. What would Lokolumbe think
if he saw me now? Viola, going to school in Maine
(capital city, Augusta).
Viola, *girl*, queen of Africa,
he would say, you made it to America!

I sit by the window with my hood
over my head, my knees to my chest.
In Maine I cannot get warm.
Why am I here and not Gwendolyn,
or my grandmother,
or Francis?
Why was the Congolese rhythm more real
when I imagined it,
walking on the Juba road?

# Barber Foods

I get a job at Barber Foods, where my mother works.
I close chicken breasts around frozen stuffing
with tiny movements of my fingers. It is not braiding,
but my fingers do this to earn money.
They call the chicken Cordon Bleu.
My mother works first shift or sometimes second shift
and drives a neighbor's Toyota to work. As a girl
she had driven my grandfather's truck
on the dusty roads of Juba, but I know
she is not used to American highways.
The African people are having too many accidents here.

I work second shift three school days and Saturdays.
At Barber Foods, I wear a blue hairnet
and huddle into my shoulders to ward off
the freezing temperature on the line. Sometimes
I am on a pretend runway with Abby,
laughing,
instead of closing chickens at Barber Foods.
I also take care of Frieda's son, Jamal.
On Saturdays I take Jamal home with me
when Frieda comes to Barber Foods to work her shift.
I am so cold when I come off the line.
I feel like I will freeze that child
if I hold him too close to my chest.
I think my mother makes me care for Jamal
so I will have no time to find a world away from her.

*In Africa,* she begins instructions.
*In Africa,* no person is left to eat alone.
Did you wash the chicken?
*In Africa,* a daughter never forgets to cook.
She is afraid that I will leave her
to go to the mall with Jackie
and Poni who even has a car
that she drives like a warrior.
Maybe if Francis were with us,
my mother would let a little bit of me be in Maine.
I earn $6.25 an hour at Barber Foods.
I use the money to buy our food.
But even when I work till midnight,
I do my homework almost till the morning.
Habuba would be proud.

# Africa Magic

I have one! I have my own phone card!
I buy it at the bodega when I cash my paycheck,
the plastic card with the picture of elephants.
Now I put minutes on the silver phone from Walmart.
We hear there is a central phone building in Juba
where sometimes people come and can talk to their family
in America. I try the long chain of numbers that might
connect me to the central place where someone
might say, Yes, I saw this person, your grandmother.
I will go and tell her to come.
I call the numbers day after day. One day Jackie,
Poni, and I sit by the elephant tree in the cemetery
and I push in the long chain of numbers
and finally! a voice answers. And this person agrees
to send someone to find my grandmother.
I shout, "Put her on, put her on!" And after a very long time,
they do! Habuba's voice sounds faint, but I listen.
I shut my eyes
and I become a little child
remembering the heat of her skin.
I tell her my school has one thousand students.
"Impossible," I think she says.
"Habuba, it is very different here.
Students are supposed to talk.
My teachers want to know what I think!
I have a job."
She says she is living with Gwendolyn and her son.

He's three! I think she says, three.
I remember a frail infant born in the rain.
I remember Gwendolyn's bulging belly,
and my heart aches for the day she poured
groundnut seeds into Francis's open palms
and our family was together.
Before the phone goes dead, I say again and again,
"We will help you to get on the list for America.
Please come."

# Lucky

"Lucky," little Jamal shrieks. "Lucky rain."
"Yes, rain is good luck," I say, "In Africa."
We run through the rain from the swings
to a picnic table under an awning at the playing field.
I do not let go of Jamal's hand.
He is fast as a cheetah. I yank him
like my mother, who put up with no wiggling,
no peak-a-boo hiding with my little brother.
Suddenly, I am on the Cairo street in the dust storm
with the weight of Francis on my chest.
It comes in a flash. My muscles go weak.
But no,
I am safe on a playground in America,
and I did not bring my little brother.
I left Francis in the war.
Sorrow creeps into me
like the rain in my eyes and my mouth,
soaking into shoes.
I stop by a thin tree. I am tired. All I want
is to fall asleep and pretend I hear the sound
of my grandmother's and my mother's voices
in the courtyard.
Instead, I hear a shriek.
"Jamal!" I had let loose of his tugging hand.
It took him less than a second to run.
"Jamal!"
Ahead of me, boys, not thinking about the rain,

kick a soccer ball in the field.

I bring my body up tall and strong.

I will grab Jamal away.

Five boys. Tall like men.

Danger does not have to be in the night.

Danger can be in the light of day.

I pull my sweatshirt hood tight to my head.

Then one of the boys comes pounding toward me

and slides across the wet grass.

He has lifted Jamal and carries him on his shoulders.

The shrieks are Jamal's laughter.

Still, I back up as the boy races

across the earth,

then deposits a laughing Jamal at my feet.

"You lose this kid?" the boy says.

I grab Jamal's skinny shoulders.

The boy has red hair. I know his face.

He stands before us, grinning.

"Hey, you're in my class.

This kid's a natural," he says

about Jamal's squealing sprint across the soccer field.

"Give him a few years, he can make the team."

But I am dragging a screaming Jamal home.

I mumble, "Thank you," but my heart is racing

and I run, yanking Jamal,

back in the memory

of footsteps pounding,

falling across my own in Juba red dirt.

# Beauty

I am drawn to things that have beauty.
I want a butterfly tattoo on my shoulder.
I'd like to wear a tight, silver evening gown
that scoops across my front like the model Alek Wek.
One night my mother is getting ready to go out.
She and Frieda are going to hear the Congolese musician
Kanda Bongo Man at the Center for Cultural Exchange.
She wears an African dress that is red and orange
with golden shapes of girls, their arms swaying in the air.
My mother wears tight rows
she plaited around the crown of her head.
She wears sandals that glitter and drop
sequins wherever she goes.
I tease her about showing off her ankles in this dress.
"You are in America now," I nearly sing to my mother.
"You can wear anything."
"*Un lo ki lú*, Let God strike me dead!" she laughs.
"If you can wear a dress to there,
then I can wear a dress to here,"
I call back, touching my hip bone.
Tonight my mother and I are like sisters
when it comes to beauty.

# Soccer Team

Half of the soccer team is African boys.
And also the boy who carried Jamal
on his shoulders—he is on the team.
He is Andrew, the fisherman in my cooking class.
When the African boys come to tease the girls,
Andrew comes too.
Jackie is so American,
she takes a puff of a cigarette.
Andrew teases me about English words
that make no sense.
He says, "I'm kidding you,
and a baby goat's a kid.
Then there's that kid I met, Jamal."
He spins the ball, and I learn
all the kinds of "kids" my mother does not know.
If I tried to explain this distinction to my mother,
she would only say,
"Where do we buy this baby goat?
You will cook it on Sunday."
To my mother, English is spoken when useful.
To me she speaks Arabic.

Also, this boy Andrew has a truck. He owns it.
My mother is driving on the interstate
without knowing the laws, only go and stop.
Even Frieda does not know, but everyone
drives in America.

I think about Andrew's big purple truck
he leaves in parking lots and on curbs.
I imagine practice driving it.
Then I could teach my mother
the meaning of the signs beside the road
and help her get a license.
I could also learn some better words from this American.
Mrs. Mejía would press her hands to her heart and say,
"Viola, your English astounds me."

# Telephone Calls

Andrew calls my house on Monday.
My mother does not let me talk to him.
She tells him,
"Do not call my house again."
To me she says,
"Why does this boy call you?"
"He wants to get the homework assignment," I say.
"Tell him, do not call here.
You cannot tell him the homework.
Tell him he should get the homework at school."
Andrew calls on Tuesday.
He tells me next day in cooking class.
Something about him teases
a smile from the corner of my lips.
"Hello, this is Andrew," he explains that he says.
"May I please talk to Viola?"
"No boy can call this house!" my mother says.
"No boy. She cannot talk."
And she hangs up.

That night my mother sits with me.
She says my hair is longer.
She will oil the patchy place in the back.
She is going to plait me in the front
because these tiny braids protect the hair.
I do not say no to my mother, even for this.
We sit and watch TV, and she oils my hair.

I feel her fingers work, right to the middle,
left to the middle, grab the hair under.
She makes a dozen lines across the crown of my head.
While she is braiding, it is like Francis is here.
Feeling my mother's fingers brings him back, and we
laugh a little at how we can slip into Africa when
it is just her and me and not my friends
who smell of American food.

I try to forget the things I know that my mother
does not know. Mrs. Mejía saying if girls study,
they can have the world; a place Poni tells about
where I can get a tattoo on my shoulder blade;
a boy who can teach me to drive.
But I cannot forget.

Now I sleep in my separate small bed.
Jackie has Michael Jackson on her bedroom wall.
When we cook together, she blasts the words to
"The Way You Make Me Feel."
I think of decorations I might hang on my walls
and wonder, if I did talk to Andrew on the phone,
what would we say?

# How to Talk to a Boy You Have Use Of

Two days later, Andrew comes to my house.
I look past him,
and there is the big purple truck by our curb.
I am off today, and my mother is at work.
It is 4 o'clock. She will return at 6:00.
My heart races, part fear, part joy that
I could even hope to drive his truck.
"Come in," I say, real soft, like a lady
in Africa would talk to a guy she has use of.
I leave the door open.
Andrew comes in and he looks so funny
sitting on my mother's lace-fringed couch
that suddenly I see how African our house is,
the beads draping the doorways,
the tall giraffe beside the TV,
the incense burning.
Is he laughing?
I go to prepare a tray as my mother
would do for guests in Africa.
I drop a stick of cinnamon in the electric pot
and boil the water. I set cookies on the gold-rimmed dish.
I pour water over the tea in the cup.
I bring these things to Andrew,
who sits with his mouth open,
taking in the room,

in a baseball cap that says "Let Me Fish,"
his red hair jutting out from all sides.
"Is this African?" he says about the tea.
"No, from Stop and Shop."
"No shit," he says. "Tastes like African."
Then I get scared.
What have I done, to let him inside?
I cannot tell him what it looks like to the community.
Even the truck.
I remember Juba.
How word spread like drumbeats:
*Viola has lost her bride wealth.*
But we are in America,
and this boy can teach us how to drive.
I stand up,
terrified my mother will come home early.
"Do you have a license?" I ask.
"What do you think, I'm illegal?"
"I need to learn how to drive by the law," I say.
I look out the door, frightened
I will see my mother's blazing eyes.
"Can't right now. We're going fishing tonight.
How 'bout tomorrow?"
Andrew stands up. He is good at taking hints.
"I don't have a car," I say.
"All the better," he says. "You can learn on Sally.
Nothin' you can do hasn't been done to that truck."
Andrew eats all the cookies and empties the cup.
"I'll give you a call when we get in."
He walks in giant steps past the satellite dish

and leaps into Sally. I suck in my breath,
not sure who I fear most: Andrew,
or my mother knowing
I talked to him in her house.

# Snow

Several African mothers stand in the white
that is falling from the sky.
My mother says I cannot go to school. It is not safe.
I am ready with my coat and hood and book bag
on my shoulder. "I have to go to school."
It is January and we are having final exams,
but even this fact does not persuade her.
My mother will not go to work.
Miss America Abby has told me
snow can fall heavy like this snow.
When I tell my mother, one African mother says,
"Yes, sometimes this happens."
Many children are kept out of school. They are running,
playing in the snow, and their mothers cannot
make them go back inside.
I call Abby to come,
explain again to my mother. While I wait for Abby,
I listen to the mothers talk.
"Never has a child talked back to me as they do here."
"My son said to me, 'In Sudan, the parents beat us
all the time. Here they cannot beat us.'"
"How can we raise our children here?"

Abby pedals up on a bicycle. She joins the African
mothers standing in the snow.
A yellow cap with tassels hides Abby's red-streaked curls.
Everyone politely shakes Abby's hand. She laughs,

"How do you do." "Nice to meet you."
"Thank you for inviting me."
Her blue jacket sparkles like the snow.
"Please," my mother says, "come in."
"Tell them I have to go," I say, stepping away.
"Tell them what you said about the snow."
She turns to my mother. "Yes, you can walk on it."
She says many footprints of boots make a path through it.
We gaze up into the sky that seems to have dropped
nearer our heads. Abby explains the danger of ice.
"That's when you have to be careful," she says.
With their shoes the mothers test the snow for ice.
"No, not now," Abby assures. "This is powder. Beautiful,
light powder. Not ice. It's easy to shovel."
"Mrs. Mejía is waiting for me," I say, anxious.
"I have English and history tests. I have studied all night.
At this moment, I know Langston Hughes
by heart. If I wait, I might forget."
The mothers shake their heads but do not stop me.
Abby goes inside with my mother and the others.
They will eat sambusas and drink sweet milky tea
while I race down Abby's bicycle track and make
my own deep footprints in the snow.

# House Rules

My cousin Jackie comes over.
She wants me to do micro braids in her hair.
No African girl does not know how to braid hair.
She says I am lazy. She sits on the edge of the bed
and rubs oil into the back of her hair.
In the mirror I see I wear a crooked smile.
"Mrs. Mejía said I will move from beginner ESL
to intermediate literature studies, maybe advanced."
"You are on a fast track," Jackie says,
her face bent down to her chest.
Something else makes me smile. Andrew will
teach me how to drive stick shift very soon.
Jackie knows.
I whisper, "Andrew has not been in class.
I wish he could call."
"My boyfriend called," Jackie says in her sly way.
She raises her head, opens her arms dramatically.
"My mom picked up. He said, 'How are you, Auntie?
Are you having a nice day?'"
Jackie chats while she works the oil,
but I worry my mother can hear.
"He is like real polite," Jackie continues.
"But she would not let me talk to him."
While she tells this, her fingers glisten with oil.
"He called another time," Jackie says.
"Mom picked up and he said,
'Hello, Auntie, are you having a nice day?

Can I talk to Jackie?' very polite.
and Mom called me. 'Jackie,' and she held out the phone.
'Here is a *boy* for you.'"


My mother stops at the doorway.
She sees our smiles. She has heard us talking.
Her strong hands grasp the door frame.
A printed scarf frames the wide bones
of her face.
"If you try to meet with a boy,"
 she says softly,
"I will say, *There* is the door. *Go.*
I will give you a ticket to Africa
if you do not want to live by the rules."
"Oh, you are a tough one,"
Jackie teases my mother,
cocking her head.
But my mother does not smile.
I remember my mother when the soldier
shoved the sack of sugar at her.
She tried to keep her bony ribs between
me and him. She did not bend
her straight back because he had a rifle.
I know how strong she is.
But would she send me back to the war?
I try to imagine waking up on my mat
if I lived in Juba, and I could hear Habuba
humming and smell soot from the cooking stove.
Then feel the ground shake when mortars fall
and feel the terror for my family.

I wish I could see my grandmother's bright eyes.
I have been here less than a year,
yet I do not think I can be all Sudanese, all the time.
Already, am I part American?
I don't feel like any one thing.
"She is all African,"
I tell Jackie when my mother leaves
to listen to Al Jazeera.
Jackie agrees, "She's not split like you and me.
She said that because she's afraid.
Mothers don't send their kids back to the war."

Once more I am in the desert where I
walked with Lokolumbe.
It was simpler then.
Work, sleep, and wait,
but then we knew what we were waiting for—
a visa.
Here, I study very hard. I have five library books.
We are busy, busy, busy. I earn $6.25 an hour.
But I am still waiting.
I am waiting to feel alive.
I am waiting for myself
to catch up with
my body.
My mother
holds me tight.

# Foods A-Z: Pie

Yes, I do go to Andrew's house in the East End.
I know what I vowed on the train beside Francis,
that I would find us a way to be free in America.
I tell Francis that I'm helping us to be free.
I'm inviting this American to help our family.
My mother, she must never know.
In Africa, we do not do this,
but I need to learn to drive.
My skin quivers in the cold.
I bury my face in the hood of my coat
and watch for Andrew's truck on the street
and his voice calling out,
"Halloooo."
I do not think of my mother's steel eyes.


I know which house is his. Jackie showed me.
So when I see the brick house
with the blue door,
and Sally pulled in front,
two tires over the curb,
I stop. It is snowing.
Andrew must have seen me.
He opens the blue door.
"You are not coming to school," I say.
He watches me and a smile comes into his eyes.
"Couldn't make it," he says.
He looks at me, his arms hanging from the door frame.

"What are you cooking these days?" he says.

I hand him a slice of pie, still warm, wrapped in foil.

"Thanks." He takes the slice,

which he unwraps and eats in two bites

while the snow falls lightly on my braids.

"Andrew!" I hear a voice from inside, low and insistent.

"Andrew!" Andrew doesn't answer. He says to me,

"Been out fishing. I'm always beat."

"Beat?"

"Need some shut-eye." He drops his eyelids

over his green eyes, lets his body sag,

then his eyes smile on me.

"It's okay, it helps Mom out. Earning some cash."

"Andrew!" from inside.

"I better go," I say.

"Andrew, invite her in. You got a friend?

Let the girl in."

Andrew shrugs. "My mom," he says.

"You probably don't want to come in."

I shake my head.

A television blasts from the next room.

I hear a thump, like a chair has been knocked over.

A frown clouds his eyes.

"She's not feeling good—my mom," he says.

He brushes snow from the rows

my mother has tied in my hair.

I draw away, although the touch was kind,

then turn and race into the snow as his mother

calls once more.

"Great pie," he shouts.

"Blueberries," I shout back.
"Not fishing tomorrow," he says.
Running feels good.
I remember my grandmother praising,
*You have long legs for running.*
I can choose to run—or stay.

# Flea Market

I meet Andrew at the playing field.
Sally idles, loud and smoky.
First I sit behind the wheel to learn the buttons
and the gears.
"Okay, let's get you good at shifting," he says.
I shove the clutch with my left foot.
Shift, one, two, three, four, reverse.
Twice I turn on the windshield wipers.
"You learn this, you can buy any model on the lot,"
Andrew says.
Andrew's hair looks fluffy. He's not wearing his cap.
He parts it on the right, but it doesn't want to do that,
and some of it floats up when he talks.
I find myself leaning in to study his hair.
Habuba has never seen hair like this.
What would she think?
I practice and practice and practice
till I feel new muscles in my arm.
"Ey, too many buttons," I say.
"Break time," he says. "You ever been to a flea market?"
"Fleas, no, we do not have them."
"Not fleas," he says. He explains these fleas,
and we are laughing. I ride with Andrew to the market.
It is a sprawling open market
like the Cairo souq,
only without camels and goats,
and it is in a building.

Andrew and I *pool our change* and
*buy the town*, as he says.
We buy matching fur hats for 50¢ and
pretend we are from Russia,
a red-headed boy who smells like fish
and a girl who is as skinny
as the Nile on a map of Africa.
I jump and skip to fight the cold.
Andrew doesn't wear gloves.
His calloused baseball-mitt hands
do not seem to feel the cold.
"I collect egg beaters," he says.
"For when you are a chef?" I say.
"Maybe," he says, "but I just like egg beaters.
There's a million kinds of gear action.
What do you collect?"
"Nothing," I say.
"Sure you do. You just don't know what it is yet."
We pass seas of tables with glass beads, shells,
and brilliant stones; baths for birds;
a poster of cats on strike because they want cream
and not milk; fancy clothes we hold up to each other.
And then, a necklace with seven tiny bronze elephants.
I pick up the elephants and feel their weight in my palm.
It is the first thing I touch that makes me
think of a place in America as well as in Africa.
"Sold," Andrew says, "to the girl in the Russian hat."
From then on, we search for egg beaters and elephants
until we run out of quarters.
On the way home we listen to my CD of Koffi Olomide

and his African drums,
Andrew drumming on the steering wheel
and me dancing with my arms in the air,
holding one of Andrew's new egg beaters.
For a minute I am on the edge of knowing who I am,
I mean, feeling in the place where I actually am,
flying on the highway in America:
a Russian girl and owner of elephants.

# People of the Rain

A cold rain is falling, and Andrew and I watch it.
We also watch the clock in my apartment
for when my mother's borrowed Toyota
will pull into the parking lot.
I tell Andrew,
"My mother and I are people of the rain.
We are sisters of snakes."
I tilt my head back and laugh.
"Sometimes the snakes are down on the floor.
We don't hurt them. They are kind.
If somebody is dead in the house,
the cobras stay behind the bed. They stay
with the body. They mourn.
When rain comes, so do the cobras.
Where the snake is, the rain is.
They are lucky."
"So," Andrew says, "you're a good luck girl.
I'm pretty superstitious myself."
And then I cover my mouth to hold back my laughs.
"My grandmother believes that
about the snakes," I say.
"I believe it a little. If I found a cobra in the cupboard,
I would not be afraid.
The only thing I am afraid of here are cops.
They remind me of soldiers, like in Sudan."
I am stretched out, curved over the couch,
my head propped on my arm.

"I would like you to see the Africa moon," I say.
But I cannot tell him about my country's war.
I cannot tell him about the minefields
and how no one could grow food,
only small miracles like Gwendolyn's groundnuts.
He cannot know how easy it is to throw away a girl
like me.
Does he know things that bring terror?
The twirl of a boy's body when he is shot.
The tobacco smell of a soldier's breath.
Francis in his Magic Kingdom T-shirt,
my eyes demanding *silence*!
And still I could not protect him.
The weight of his small body on my chest.
Later the loss of everybody but my mother,
and my terror that my mother might
send me
away from her.
I don't tell him that I keep a book from Africa,
my grandmother's hymnal,
under my pillow.
Andrew's burly face is worried as he
watches for my mother's car.
He stands.
All I say is,
"In Africa the moon fills the sky."

# White Girl's Braids

My friend Lado—who comes to watch the war
at our house because we have the dish—
works in his mother's restaurant,
Ezo African Restaurant.
There he meets lots of girls, even white girls.
He wants to bring a white girl over for us
African girls to braid her hair.
Poni says she is definitely *not* going to braid
a white girl's hair,
and we burst out laughing at Lado and his girls.
Sudanese girls keep stopping by my apartment
one Saturday, until a roomful of girls
are lounging on the sofa and chairs,
our legs slung over each other's.
Koffi's drums pound from the TV.
"You know in a salon, it costs $500 for the braids,"
I say about doing the white girl's hair.
"It takes from 9 in the morning until 4.
Lado's friend could go there."
I am wearing capri pants and a string top
like some other girls. We pretend we are glamorous.
Even though it's only spring outside,
inside we keep it summer.
"She is not even Lado's girlfriend," Jackie says.
We groan.
"The white girl has some other African boyfriend,
and she wants to surprise him with African braids."

"Ummmph," the girls say.
I cannot imagine the feel of smooth, white-girl hair
between my fingers. My friends laugh.
How could a white girl know
how only someone you trust should braid your hair,
how someone bad could work magic against you?
How could a white girl know
what the braid means to an African man?
How a braid factors into the girl's value as a bride,
her beauty and quick tongue,
her education,
her prospects as a mother.
Her virginity.
All these things add value.
How can this white girl know?

# We Do Not Do This in Africa

I hear mothers talking as they work on the line.
*"Here I see the white girls have no shame."*
*"This is true. One time a boy came*
*and kissed my niece on the mouth.*
*I said to her, please, please do not do this.*
*I have younger children here who can see.*
*We do not do this in Africa."*
*"Most of our children now do the American way,*
*and we have lost our dignity. If she is going to marry,*
*how can she have a boyfriend?"*
*"If a daughter gives herself away,*
*this is like killing the mother,*
*because the daughter is her only wealth."*

That is what the mothers believe.

It is dangerous to even meet with Andrew.
But he can help me learn American skills
for driving on the highway.
And if I have an American friend,
I might wake up feeling like I live in Maine
instead of waking up *every* morning in Africa.

# Abby's Advice

"You could go down the highway together
to Old Orchard Beach
where sometimes African girls
hang out with white boys.
Old Orchard is a wild mix of beach shops
and signs that say *Nous Sommes Français*
to invite the French Canadians.
Past the motels and shops is the wild ocean.
Your mom would probably never go there.
An African girl could walk with a boy on 5th Street,
where vendors sell tattoos
and orange Creamsicles
and you can get Caribbean hair wraps.
You could laugh together,
and maybe Andrew could take your hand."

# Stick Shift

I wear a new yellow shirt and over it
the gray sweatshirt jacket that I nearly
always wear. We are out past the AAA office
and the U-Haul renting company,
on the edge of the city.
"I remember how to steer," I say.
"Piece a cake, then," Andrew says.
The truck is already running and
I remember the gears: 1, 2, 3, 4, reverse.
I grasp the stick and
shove it into first.
"A little gas," Andrew says.
We leap forward.
I see a red stop sign.
"You might want to slow up," Andrew says.
"Oh," I say.
I am focused on my left foot on the clutch
while my right foot moves between the brake and the gas.
"We're rolling," Andrew says.
I squeeze the hand brake.
"Ohhhhhh," I exhale softly.
My fingers curl over the brake handle.
"Give 'er some gas," he says.
The truck's front tire is stuck in a hole of broken-up tar.
"More gas?"
"Sure."
I rev the engine. The truck roars, then stalls.

I turn the key, and the truck comes back to life.
I inch forward.
The engine dies again.
And then I understand.
Get it in gear.
Foot on the gas.
Let out on the clutch.
We clear the rim of the hole.
I careen ahead, laughing.
"Stick shift," I say. "Stick shift!"
When I come to a stop,
I laugh. Proud.
Andrew pumps my hand in congratulations.
Then we run around the car,
changing places.
"I want to tell you something," he says.
He stops with his hand on the key
in the ignition.
"Your life back home where you were,
if you ever want to talk,
you can tell me.
I've been through some shit.
You won't shock me.
Just wanted to say that."
I look out at the Marginal Way,
the path by the bay where
people walk dogs and fly kites and throw Frisbees.
I shake my head. "It's a civil war.
We don't want to be Muslim, we people of the south."
He waits.

I stare at the side of his neck he calls a rugby neck.

"So many died," I tell him. "You cannot imagine
how they throw people away." He waits.

"Millions of my people."

He keeps looking forward so I cannot see his eyes.

I keep talking.

"If they did not kill you, they did other very bad things.

Things like torture. And kidnap. And rape.

A girl is very valuable as a new bride.

A girl will bring much wealth to her family."

"Already knew you were worth a lot," he says.

"Me," I say, "Not so much."

He looks at me and his forehead wrinkles
with questions he does not ask.

His eyes are brown with specks of green.

"I am no longer valuable."

"What's that mean?" he says.

I shrug. "Girls are not safe in Sudan."

Silence.

I should not have told him.

"I need to go home," I say.

"Oh, Jesus, you do," he says, checking his watch.

He turns the key with his hand
that had not moved while I talked.

Why did I tell him?

I should not have told him *that*.

Is he disgusted?

Andrew negotiates the tight streets
back to Kennedy Park.

At my apartment, I leap out of Sally.

"You better not get a lot of horsepower
when you get a car," he says.
"You'll be drag racing in the streets."
"Thank you," I say.
He pumps my hand in his funny way.
He is studying me from under his Let Me Fish cap.
His eyes are a darker green now.
"You want to study later?" he says.
"Yes," I say, surprised. "Good-bye."
"Bye."
I begin to run up our sidewalk but freeze
before I come to the dish.
A fear shoots through my chest.
How careless. How *stupid*.
The blue Toyota my mother drives is already there.

# Part Three
## *Elephant Songs*

Portland, Maine
United States

2003

# War

*Now the war comes back to me.*

*Again, there is only the war.*

My mother holds my arm and wrist
over the boiling water
in a grip that feels like death.
I yell out.
But I cannot escape. She is very strong.
My hand begins to throb with the heat.
"Mother, don't hurt me.
You are hurting me!" I scream.
"You cannot go with this boy," she commands.
"Yumis! Mommy, let me go."
My hand, it hurts worse than any other pain.
I think, *Oh, God, she will kill me.*
First my hand, then my face, then all of me.
"Yumis!"
She has the strength of rage.
I scream.
I cannot see my hand in the steam.
She wants to put my hand in the boiling water
like I saw Andrew do to small monsters
with claws from the sea.
"Yumis!
My hand, you are killing me."
"You kiss that boy. I see you kiss him."
My hand is bright red. I see it now.

It is the world, my hand.
"I did not kiss him!"
"You bring us shame!" my mother yells.
Jamal must have heard my screams.
He has come into the kitchen with Dursu,
the neighbor girl, to see what is happening.
Dursu has been to school where her
teacher—like mine—taught her
the emergency number.
"Dursu!" I cry, "Call 911!"

# Burn

I am lying on the fish and moonbeam tiles
of the kitchen floor
when I hear the banging, banging, banging.
My hand betrays me.
I cannot stop the shrieks from my throat.
My mother is stretched on the sofa beneath
the photograph of my father
and the photograph of my brother.
She calls out for people to enter,
the Sudanese coming to gather.
She does not look worried,
only exhausted.
She had just worked twelve hours on the line.
Two soldiers enter.
No.
Uniforms. Portland Police Department.
One is a woman.
She tells me her name—Sergeant Linda Johnson.
She is leaning over me.
"Where do you hurt?"
I only open my mouth and gasp in air and cry.
She cannot miss the color that is not human.
"Did your mother do this?"
My mother, she paces up and down the hall.
"She is my daughter," my mother says.
"Get out of my house."
Outside, lights flash.

The lady still leans in to me.
"Tell us what happened.
Did your mother burn you?"
I am still screaming with my hand held high.
"She burn me. She burn me!"
A man with a furry beard reaches for my hand,
but I am screaming—he looks like a soldier!
This man wears a badge with the letters EMT.
He fills a basin with water. I see
my hand palm up in the blue basin.
A third person takes my mother by the elbows.
I bolt up and run to her.
"Mother!
I only called 911 to stop the burning!"
With my good hand,
I grab at my mother, her arm.
Then I am on the floor trying to grasp her leg.
It takes all the people to pull me from her.
"You cannot take my mother!"

And then I am alone
with these strangers. Jamal
peeks in at us; Dursu is a guard,
her hands on her child hips.
My mother is gone.
"Where is my mother?" I say.
"I'll tell you after the judge talks to her.
She can't do this," Linda Johnson says,
as if to a child.
She leads me to the couch,

places my hand in the basin again.
"You do not understand, in Africa—"
"She is not in Africa."
Jamal enters and climbs into my lap.
I can barely see my hand—
like a fish in the basin—
through the blur in my eyes.
Jamal is silent, watching every move
the policewoman makes. The man with the beard
wraps the blood pressure cuff over my arm,
places a thermometer under my tongue.
Linda Johnson sits in the chair.
She is writing.
She has long, thin fingers that hold a yellow pen.
"Find my cell," I say to Dursu.
But I do not need to call anyone. Soon
the aunts and elders from Juba begin to arrive,
and they are on their cell phones to Africa.
They try to reach Juba to tell them
*Tereza is gone with the police.*
Linda Johnson writes in her book.
"Can you walk to the ambulance?" she asks.
She sits beside me. I shiver. It is dusk.
I force my mind to focus on the fading light.
It is that lost time when morning is coming in Africa,
but here we're not yet in the dark of the night.
"How bad is it?" she says.
But I do not talk, I only try to
hold the tears back
while I sit still as an elephant.

The pain grips my hand and pulses
like electric shocks to my heart
and my belly.
Linda Johnson slips the yellow pen between
the fingers of my left hand.
"Sign this," she says.
"I wrote down what I saw here.
Has your mom done this before?
You must tell us what your mom did
so she can never do this to you again."
I do not take the pen.
Who is Linda Johnson to decide about my mother?
"Who is next of kin?"
Linda Johnson's eyes scan the line of women.
Any woman from Juba is my aunt and next of kin.
They listen in silence
while Linda Johnson explains the law.
"You can't protect someone who hurts her child."
The aunts from Juba talk among themselves in Arabic
and consult with family in Cairo and St. Paul.
One aunt, Lado's mother, tries to explain
to Linda Johnson. "You see," she says in her soft,
melodic tone, "all the mothers discipline their children.
In our families it is the mother who decides."

"Come on, now," Linda Johnson says.
"The ambulance is taking you to the hospital."
I shake my head.
"You need a doctor to treat this."
The aunts, including Aunt Rita, sit beside me.

The bearded man pulls out a handkerchief
and wipes sweat from his forehead and neck.
"The department will bring in the African elders,"
he says to Linda Johnson. "They'll be part of this."
Linda Johnson raises both of her hands to the air.
Maybe she is a musician with those beautiful hands.
"You have to go; it's the law," she says.
Rita rises. She pulls my arm and I rise.
They put me in the ambulance, and all I can say is,
"My mother,
where is she?"

# Doctor

My whole palm and my fingers swell with blisters.
*Hold on. Don't give in to the pain.*
I think I see my grandmother there,
squatting by the cook fire.
Then I see my mother telling me,
*Hurry, fill the can with water,*
and she's laying out her beads
for the ladies in our courtyard.
At the hospital, I cry silently when the doctor
touches me. He gives me something for my
terrible pain. "I have to go to work,"
I tell the doctor.
"I must earn the money."
His eyes move from my hand to my face.
He wears a baggy suit
that droops off his shoulders.
His eyes shine, like he has a secret
and he cannot wait to tell it.
"What kind of work?" he asks.
With my left hand, I show him the small
movement I make with my fingers to close the
chicken and how quick the chickens,
sometimes tumbling, come down the belt.
"You can't do that job anymore," he says.
"You can't put on gloves."
"How will I tell my supervisor?" I say.

"We will call them," he says. And then,
seeing the necklace I'd forgotten I am wearing,
"Nice elephants." He recites:
"Elephants are lovely guys,
They're good and true and tell no lies."
A slight smile curves his lips.
I let my eyes close for a second.
I feel the still, gray presence of the elephant.
I feel its breath on my face.
The doctor talks on, his head slightly bowed,
peering up at my face over his glasses.
His voice is raspy, and every few words
he clears his throat.
"I'm going to give you a splint.
*kh-hem kh-hem.* You won't like it now,
but this'll keep you from getting a claw hand."
"What is a claw hand?" I say.
He curves his fingers and pretends they become a
cat's claw poised to catch a bird.
His old blue eyes squint at me.
"We have to protect your tendons," he says,
"*kh-hem,* so you can spread your fingers long
and when you go to your prom you will have
only a small scar and your hand will grasp
your bouquet with no problem."

I have heard of proms.
A flash of Andrew comes to me.
He is in a tuxedo. I am in a silver gown.

"Sit still," the doctor says.
"First we give you the miracle medicine.
Silver sulfadiazine."
His eyes are kind and the pain medicine is working.
I like the word *silver*. I shut my eyes and see it glitter.
I begin to be able to fill my lungs, then slowly . . .
exhale.
He squeezes medicine on my palm
and for a few minutes I do not worry
about not filling my place on the line
or how to save money for a car
or my mother.
The doctor gently opens my hand.
He splints my wrist up and over to my thumb
so I will not have a claw.
I shut my eyes again.
The doctor is still talking. I am near sleep.
I mumble, holding on to his rhyming words,
"Elephants are lovely guys . . .
and don't tell lies."

"Let her sleep," I hear the doctor say
as he shuffles out the door. And then he says,
"Is DHHS involved?"
"Yes," comes the reply, "and the elders
of the Sudanese community are counseling the family."
"I hope to God they know what they're doing,"
the doctor says.
"I never want to see another girl like this."

# I Will Braid Your Hair

Marko comes to the hospital, and he and Auntie
take me home. Marko says that my mother
will talk to a judge in the morning.
When they meet it is called an arraignment,
and many elders from the community will tell about
us fleeing the civil war and say
the judge should not punish my mother.
Then Marko describes a caseworker,
someone who says I can't live alone with my mother,
if the judge allows her to come home.
*I can't live with my mother?*
The caseworker assigned Frieda, Jamal's mom,
to be my guardian.
When I get home, Frieda and Jamal
have moved into my mother's house.
This is how it would be in Africa.
We would all be together.
What I need, though, is my mother.
I wait up through this night before the arraignment.
I try to go to the bathroom
with my right hand in a splint and bandage.
I am wearing the yellow shirt with bell sleeves
and the same tight jeans I wore
to learn stick shift with Andrew.
I wrestle with my jeans using my one hand,
ashamed that I cannot do this

and not spill my urine on the floor
we keep immaculate.


In the morning, Josephine, the elder
who runs the restaurant and my friend Lado's mother,
brings my mother home from the judge.
My mother steps out of Josephine's car.
Her body moves slowly up the walk.
Her mouth droops.
Inside, Josephine says to me and Frieda,
"The elders have custody on this offence.
We told the judge her long story, of the war in Juba,
the escape to Khartoum,
the hopeless years in Cairo.
She is still grieving for her husband and her son.
We told him all this."
My mother sinks down upon the couch.
Josephine continues,
"The judge gives one chance to the community."
My mother glances at me
but does not seem to see me.
Josephine's gaze sweeps from Frieda, to my mother,
to me.
She says, "Later we will talk," and she is gone.
My mother lies down on the sofa.
With my good hand, I make her a cup of tea
but she does not drink. So I sit by her.
She clicks the remote,
and we watch news from the Cairo station.
They show Somali soldiers

raising their weapons in salute to the camera.
I think of Andrew and me
in Russian hats at the flea market.
Why did I think I could be that girl?
My mother sleeps.
I whisper to my sleeping mother,
"When you are awake, I will braid your hair."

# Ezo

I stay close to my friends
Jackie and Poni.
Jackie says I should call Andrew,
tell him about my mom and Linda Johnson.
Tell him why I'm not at school. I never do.
He would have heard what happened to me.
Everyone at school knows. I have not been to school
since the hospital. I don't care about school.
How many weeks? Two? Three? I'm not sure.
Not only am I missing Foods A–Z part 2,
I am missing Mrs. Mejía's literature studies.
I don't let myself think of her face,
which will droop in disappointment.
She thought I was a star when I told her about the
Viola and Lokolumbe English Night School
and recited "There Was a Child Went Forth"
by Walt Whitman.


When Andrew does not come,
I know it is because of what I told him
that happened to me in the war.
Before, I wanted to be American.
Now, if someone asks, I say I am Sudanese.
I say, I love my tribe.
I hang out with Lado and my people
at Ezo African Restaurant.
On the walls are batik fabric elephants,

hangings made from dried banana leaves.
They picture African women carrying baskets,
their arms stretched long above their heads.
I run the cash register with one hand.
I set up the tables. When it is busy, I bus.
But I do not cook because
I will not get near the stoves.
I earn only a little money,
just some of Lado's tips.
But here is where I want to be.


The afternoon is very quiet at the restaurant.
I daydream, looking out the window
onto Oak Street.
I read the letters
"Ezo African Restaurant"
painted over the long neck of a giraffe.
Is that Andrew's red hair and cap, his
worried face looking at me
between the backward letters?
I am excited, then terrified.
Will I have to send him away?
News will travel from the cook to my mother
instantly. I cannot risk it.
But I am wrong. It is only a fantasy Andrew.
Another day I am on the phone by the register
writing a take-out order.
I look up from the cash register.
There he is—the fantasy Andrew—with his green eyes
and the shoulders

I have lain my head against.
His grin spreads across his solid, square face.
His eyes drop to my hand,
which is still splinted and bandaged.
*Jesus!* he says.

But the real Andrew never comes,
and I do not have to send him away.

# Habuba

Lado is a talker and a girl charmer.
He's the boy who wants us girls to braid
the white girl's hair.
He's in the kitchen with a phone to his ear,
which is no surprise. That's how he usually looks.
But this time he turns to me while he talks,
and my heart starts to race.
He shakes his head that he shaved bald
for the soccer season. "Hey, she is here," he says.
He comes around the counter, holds out his phone.
I'm aware of the African designs on his shirt
—bold yellow and black—
as he moves beside me.
I put the phone to my ear. I hear,
"Little sister, Viola, how are you? This is Gwendolyn.
How are you?" she says again.
"Gwendolyn!" I cry out. "Do you have a phone?"
"For a minute," she says. "Call me back at this number."
I leave Lado's phone on the counter,
pull mine from my pocket.
I punch in the numbers for the PIN
on my African Dream card.
The international code, the continent, my country.
I feel so happy. I forget to worry.
I am calling Gwendolyn.
Yearning washes through me.
I place myself in my own courtyard in Juba,
where the moon would be up in the wide, dark sky.

I long to smell the earth by the Nile.
I sit in an empty booth beneath the wall
with the elephant picture. The elephant is young,
with ears flopping backward.
"Gwendolyn," I nearly sing,
"How old is your baby? Has the rain started?
Is my grandmother there, too? Can we talk?" I remember
Poni, South Sudan's first lady-president-to-be, singing
"South Sudan all day everyday till the day I die,"
and at this moment, I feel like singing those words, too.
"My baby is too small, Viola.
But he will be four by the end of this year, yes?
Today they give us milk, so he is peaceful.
But the war planes have not stopped for seven days.
Many of us have moved into your mother's house,
and we share what rations we have."
"But you have a phone!" I say.
She does not talk about the phone. She begins again,
"Sad news, Viola. We lived with your grandmother
for many months. She has been a grandmother to my son.
She began to sleep many hours in the day,
and it was hard for her to take a breath."
I can see Habuba with her green scarf draped
around her head when we went to get water.
The ends of the scarf flowed around her. One hand
held the water jug on her head and the other hand,
veined and thick, hung free in the tail of the scarf.
"She is strong," I say. "She will make your baby fat."
"I am trying to tell you," Gwendolyn says.
"Habuba wanted to be with you.

All the time she talked about you.
She heard that families send movies of their
children's graduation in America."
I cringe. I no longer go to school.
How could I ever tell Habuba
I'm not going to have a graduation?
"Where is she?" I begin . . .
but then I know
why Gwendolyn is calling.
"I'm very sorry, Viola. She was not strong enough."
"*No!*" I cry out.
"She wanted to stay alive to hear
you are a graduating girl."
*No.*
I always thought somehow
I would see her again.

Lado's mother, Josephine, needs to talk to Gwendolyn,
then Lado again, then the cook, and the waiter—
they pass the phone with this
news of my grandmother,
the oldest woman back in Juba.

I call my mother's number. She is on break at work,
and she answers, "Ey."
I hear in her voice what life has taught:
when news comes, do not expect it to be good.
My mother is strong. She does not cry out.
There are many relatives she will call
while I think of the elephants keening,
resting their trunks on the body of the one who has died.

# Roots

That night we go to the house of
Uncle Marko, Habuba's oldest son.
Many Sudanese come.
We stay together until late into the night.
People won't leave our family to be alone.
Jackie and I retreat into her bedroom.
"How is your mom?" Jackie says.
I shrug. "She doesn't talk to me."
"Give her time. At least the state sent Frieda
to live with you. She's young and not so strict."
Then the mothers come in and scold us:
*Serve the elders. Wash the dishes.*
We wash the dishes in Marko's American sink
with water running from a pipe, but all the time,
I think of Habuba. I always thought
she would somehow live in Kennedy Park.
She would walk this sidewalk with me to school
and in her formal way shake my teacher's hand.
Though I could not imagine how she would ever walk
the footsteps we walked to become refugees.

Outside yellow petals of May flowers
lie like a curtain on the blacktop.
And violet flowers—their color is almost like my name—
bloom outside Marko's kitchen window.
Their scent enters on the breeze.
It is the saddest sweetness I have ever smelled.

I scrub the pot with my good hand.
I think this is the smell in America that will always,
from today on, remind me of my grandmother.
The smell says to me,
*Mata nasitu wara*—Don't forget your roots.

# Mrs. Mejía Who Gave Me Three Things

The next morning, I do not get up.
I am sick. My mother says nothing
and goes to work.
I lie with the smell of the sweet terrible sadness.
I have missed all my schoolwork for three weeks.
I have not looked at books. I have lost my chances.
What chances did I think I could have?

That night I don't sleep.
I move from plan to plan in my head,
but each is like being tangled in the forest.
After my hand heals, I will get more hours
at the chicken factory.
People in Cairo ask us, please send money.
I will send money to the southern Sudanese.
Maybe that is all I can do.
Lokolumbe might now have a phone.
Could I call him?
No. I am not in school.
I have lived in America for a whole year,
and it is mostly sorrow. I don't want him to know.

I fall asleep on the couch in the dawn feeling
a soft American breeze.
In my sleep, I am back in Cairo.
I am walking. There are no elephants,

but my grandmother is there, and in my dream
I hear Lokolumbe. He opens his arms wide.
Yes, he says in my dream, and he swings his arm,
as if pointing to the vast sands of Egypt.
*If you look into the expanse of the desert,*
*you can see clearly into your own mind.*
Habuba and I are smiling at Lokolumbe's
wide-open arms.
When I wake up, Lokolumbe and Habuba
are so real, I expect us to keep talking
and laughing. I rise, plug in the electric kettle.
Somehow they do not sadden me.
They remain with me as I make tea,
my grandmother and my friend.
They would like Mrs. Mejía, I think,
my teacher who wears makeup like the stars
and has red pepper fingernails
and is old like my grandmother.
She made me remember when Habuba
pressed her fingers on the wide bones
that run across my cheeks and said,
"You are a daughter who learns from experience."


Suddenly, after barely sleeping all night
and not going to school for weeks and weeks,
I want to talk with Mrs. Mejía.


I shower with a plastic bag over my hand
to keep it dry.
Lying down, I pull on my jeans.

I am getting faster with one hand.
My mother is asleep. I do not wake her.
Outside it is warm. I have no coat. No books.
I run. I cross the field beyond Kennedy Park,
then run up the city street, past buses.
Past ambulances.
Past people jogging. I run. At the school,
I race up the stone steps
into this grand building where I used to go.
Some teachers watch me,
this tall girl running.
Some say, "Good morning." I run.
I run into Mrs. Mejía's room. She is not here.
Why isn't she here?
Is she not coming to school today?
I race down the hall.
There is a room I have never been in.
An office. Please, let Mrs. Mejía be in this room!
I round the corner and enter.
A photocopier spits out papers,
and shelves sag with books,
and at a desk, with her head of black hair
bent over a large book,
is Mrs. Mejía.
At first she does not look up. I let my gaze
roam through the room that is wallpapered
with maps, countries all over the world.
Like rivers among the maps are photos of students,
girls in prom gowns, students in graduation caps—
their arms around Mrs. Mejía,
soccer players, postcard pictures, a rose.

I see a vase of the same violet flowers
that bloom in Kennedy Park. Beside them, Mrs. Mejía
—always seeking to build our vocabulary—
had placed a notecard that reads *Lilacs*.
"Viola!" Mrs. Mejía sees me.
I look at her black eyes, and I am suddenly afraid.
What did I think I would do when I found her?
I've been her student for two semesters.
We have never talked about personal things.
I don't know what to say,
but I don't leave.
She rises and slides books from a second chair,
motions for me to sit.
In Sudan teachers are most honored.
Maybe I should remain standing.
Maybe this is her time to prepare for class.
"Please," she says. Her red fingernails
click on the chair's silver arm.
No words come to me.
With all these reasons not to sit, still I do.
My legs are long, and I can't think where to put them
till I cross them, stretched beneath her desk.
I focus on her fingernails. They are like music.
Then I think of why I must have come.
"Can you give me the assignments I missed?
Maybe I missed too much. But if I did come back,
I would read all the things and take all the tests."
Mrs. Mejía closes her book, lays down her pen.
Her hands lay free on her desk.
I settle more into the chair.
"Do you have your books?" she asks.

I shake my head. She pulls a copy of one text
from the stack on her desk. She flips
through the chapters. The next ten minutes
she spends telling me all the work in
literature studies and social studies I missed
and that I will have to make up—
with an extra paper besides.
And that doesn't even count math,
that is separate. Not to mention Foods A–Z. She says,
"There's reading in Foods A–Z. It's not just cooking."
Her hair bounces and seems to highlight this fact
we both know.
"If you want to earn the credits,
you *must* do all of the makeup work.
What were you thinking? You have the syllabus.
Go and do the work."
The fingernails are flying. She says nothing
of the gossip Jackie says is also flying
about me and Andrew and my mother.
I say, "Thank you."
I lift my head and look into her eyes.
I do not go. Her hands rest once more on the desk.
"Is there something else?" she says.
I begin to talk about my grandmother
and the phone call we got from Juba
while I was bussing tables at the restaurant.
Maybe my voice is shaking because Mrs. Mejía
gets up to shut the door. I can't stop talking.
I tell her that my grandmother said I was a daughter
who learned from experience and had a good mind
and long legs for running and a memory to hold

even things I didn't want to.

I say I don't know how old my grandmother was.

I pause—"My brother Francis was five."

I return to my focus on her fingernails,

then her eyes, which have become calm like a deep river.

I begin to tell her.

I had not come to tell her.

It is simply on my tongue to tell,

maybe the tongue that Habuba said

was power.

"Something happened in Juba

that causes me many problems.

Maybe because of what I did

I am bringing bad luck."

With the door to the office closed,

the sharp memory returns of waiting

for the sound of the soldier's footsteps.

I tell of this waiting to my teacher. She says,

"Would you feel safer if we open the door?"

I shake my head. "No, first let me tell."

I tell it fast. I tell about the boy from my tribe

in the street, the first time I saw the northern soldier.

I tell how later the soldier

took me behind the houses.

Mrs. Mejía listens.

Other students are now knocking,

knocking, knocking.

She does not answer.


"After he does this, he grabs coins from his pocket.

Coins my mother thinks I stole from him.

How could I?
The soldier spits on me
and throws the coins onto the dirt.
From now on, he says, I belong to him.
I am worth less than a goat.
My little brother is waiting in the road.
Before I run,
I curl around and grab the coins and dirt
into my palm."

Mrs. Mejía nods. Her shoulders sag.
Then she straightens herself.
She does not seem to care if homeroom
has started.
I say, "There is more."
She says, "Yes."
I reach up my good hand and rub
my hair pulled into a small knot.
I can barely say the words.

"It is more than one time."
My body is shaking.
"We did not escape the first time we tried.
I had to go back."

Like my mother, I am proud.
But unlike her,
tears fall down my face.
"I have talked about this with no one.
I might have talked with Habuba,

if she had come."
Mrs. Mejía closes her eyes.
"And now that I'm here . . . " I try to talk.
"I am not doing well. I am not American.
Or Sudanese.
I'm not in Sudan and not really in Maine.
Or maybe I'm in both of them
at the same time.
I'm in someplace I'm making *up*.
Even talking to you.
This story about the soldier . . .
my people
would never talk about it."
Still I go on, leaning into her.
"I don't do the Sudanese braids
in my hair we all do in my culture.
Why don't I? I don't know."
I rub my hair again. I laugh
and hold my hands out, palms open,
my body is all question.
Mrs. Mejía hands me a Kleenex.
I take one.
I put the Kleenex over my face
and drop my head to the back of the chair.
First period must have begun.

"I'm going to tell you one thing," Mrs. Mejía says.
I am glad she will talk.
It does not matter what she says.
Our voices feel like part of a song.

"I have met people from many counties at war,"
she says. "My country, too, Colombia,
is at war."
I lift the tissue off me and turn to her.
Her voice is husky and urgent, but also somehow
like notes the wind could carry.
"Rape is an act of war.
He raped you. However many times.
Rape is a weapon, and he used it on you.
The money you managed to gather,
it gave your family a chance to survive."

I sit very still.
My bandaged hand
rises and falls
on my ribs
as I breathe.
I do not judge what she says right or wrong.
I am content in this moment with the rhythm
of her voice in this place.
"One more thing," Mrs. Mejía says, now softly.
"You *do* braid.
In your very young life, you've braided together
the few good things you've been granted
so far on your journey."

My teacher gathers up a folder, notebooks,
*Introduction to Literature.*
"Stay as long as you need to compose yourself.
Then come to class," she says. "You have work to do."

# Accident on the Highway

I am going back to school. It is hard,
and I have no time to spend at Ezo.
I must do my regular homework
and my makeup homework. I'm not working
yet at the chicken factory because of my hand,
but every night I cook.
Before my mother comes home tonight,
I begin to prepare sambusas for dinner.
Jackie calls about a jeans sale at the mall.
Then I talk with southern Sudanese-4-Life Poni.
She tells me problems with her teachers
and about stupid comments from a store clerk.
"This is just like Cairo," she yells into the phone.
"Only here they have new ways to insult you."
Jackie calls back an hour later.
"Just wanted to tell you, Andrew and I
had a little talk at soccer practice.
He said he's glad you're back in school.
That's all, girl.
But I can tell you,
those dreamy eyes of his say more."

Something softens in my gut when I hang up.
I remember Andrew's dreamy eyes.
He talked to Jackie about me!
The sambusas are filled.
I slide the heavy plate by the skillet and go back

to reading my chapters.
To stay awake, I read out loud.
Before me on the couch I imagine
both Habuba and Lokolumbe listening.
In my imagination,
they have become friends.

The phone rings one more time.
I wonder if this time it might be Andrew's voice.
But it is not that kind of call.
It is a call with news,
the way all news travels
through the Sudanese apartments.
They say a Sudanese mother, traveling
on the highway, lost control of her car.
No, not in Juba. *Here!*
They say a police officer came up behind her
and the mother braked too hard and she was
spinning and kept spinning until she crashed.
They say the mother has gone to the hospital
and no one knows her name yet or how she is.
I put my arm across my chest like I am hit.
I call out to my mother, who is not here.
"Yumis? Mother!"
Now I remember she was going to the airport
after work. New people from Juba were coming.
Are the Sudanese thinking,
*Viola called 911 on her mother.*
*A daughter cannot do this to a mother.*
*And that is why her mother started spinning*
*on the highway.*

Then my mother walks in, limp with fatigue.
"Kadat is dead," my mother says.

My mother is here. She walks
to the kitchen. I see her shoes
she has left by the door. Kadat,
I repeat to myself. Charles's wife.
My mother is in the kitchen, peeling
sweet potatoes. Beside her, I rinse them.
I imagine Francis
tossing them in the pot.

Jackie and Aunt Rita, and my mother and I
cook all day in the apartment of our friend,
Kadat.
Charles sits nearby.
He wears creased trousers and a black suit jacket.
He sits by the window, and the trousers drape
his long legs, and on his thighs rest his open hands.
All afternoon  while we cook, he doesn't move
from this chair.
It is as if a baby sleeps in his large hands and—
at all costs—he cannot wake her.
Before, I had seen him only in his car repair shirt,
smelling of grease.
In Sudan, the women whisper, he drew maps of roads
he would build when peace comes
and he could study to become an engineer.

Other mothers and Charles's second wife
come and chop and fry in the small kitchen and lay

Kadat's table with food for her journey.
The elder man is here, and people sing a hymn.

> *We're not coming here for dancing.*
> *We're coming here for God.*
> *We're not coming here for singing.*
> *We're coming here for God.*

When the food is blessed, it becomes spirit food,
and people eat from the feast.
We never leave Charles and Kadat's family alone,
just as they did not leave my family alone.
Charles still has not moved. I make a cup of tea
and place it on the glass table beside him.
He looks up into my eyes.
He says, "Go to school, girl.
I hope you went back to school."
I say, "I go to school."
He lifts his cup of tea
as I do mine.


The aunts and grandmothers work in Kadat's
bedroom, deciding what to do with her things.
I walk around the house and among the mourners,
knowing it could have been my mother who was killed.
How could I live without my mother?
We have never been apart.


When I wake in the morning, my mother is cooking.
She yells to me, "Go and clean the bathroom.
What kind of daughter would leave hair in the sink?"
Even if she's yelling, I'm glad to hear her voice.

I watch my fingers swirl the cleaning pad.
I glance into the mirror and remember that girl-child
whose Habuba braided beads and cloths into her hair.
What if this girl here shaped braids in
her own hair?
For the first time, my fingers
imagine
the rhythm.

# Shift Change

My mother and I sit in the break room at Barber Foods.
My mother's shift is done,
and I've come with Frieda and Jamal to pick her up.
Frieda will start her shift,
and we will put Jamal to bed.
Cold clings to my mother, and she shivers.
I know she will shiver for an hour while
she tries to recover from packing frozen chickens all day.
A Cambodian girl dresses in the same pale blue coat,
hairnet, and rubber gloves that I wore at work.
Her mother will take home the baby who sleeps
in a car seat at their feet.
The mother opens bowls of pad thai and rice.
Dozens of people are changing shifts,
turning over children to the other parent or next caregiver,
and the smells of beans and rice with *sofrito*,
pork fried rice, pizza, chili rellenos, lemon chicken,
African chicken, and aseeda fill the room. During break,
you move from country to country with your nose.

Rain gusts in from the night as people leave.
At home in Africa, we would hear frogs
under the same round white moon.
"It is too cold," my mother says,
clutching her coat to her body.
"Do you remember how loud
the frogs croaked at home?" I say.

She pauses, as if to listen. When she does not answer,
I tell her, "If you come with me to the cemetery,
we might hear an owl call *hoooo hooooo.*"
"I remember the frogs," my mother says.
She had been thinking. Then she looks at me.
She begins to sing one of the hymns she used to sing
when she cooked aseeda with loud frogs in the background.
Her voice is quick and light.

> *Listen to my teachings and*
> *pay attention to what I say*
> *He say, I am the mighty God*
> *And I bring everlasting light.*
> *Hey!*

She sings high and sweet at a quick speed, clapping,
her elbows swinging back and forth.
Then she pulls up the hood of her coat
against the rain.
Jamal is bundled in his yellow slicker.
My mother takes his hand.
"I knew I would be the wife to your father," she says.
"I did not go with different boys.
As soon as I walked with him,
my family expected him to pay." She pauses.
"Everything is different here."
She has said this before, but now
the rage is gone from her voice.
What does she mean?
Is she saying that I can see Andrew?
I know she would never say this directly—
like Americans talk.

I say, "I will not let them arrest you again."

"They will not," she says.

We go out into the spring rain.

All through the night I hear the melody

of the hymn my mother sang:

> *Listen to my teachings and*
> *Pay attention to what I say.*
> *He say, I am the mighty God*
> *And I bring everlasting light.*

One more thing comes to me in the night:

As soon as I get my bandage off, I will find a way

to teach my mother the American rules for driving.

# My Hand

Today, I get the splint off my hand.
Slowly, I try to extend my fingers,
but the muscles are stiff, and my fingers
barely move. I must use my hand again!
I press and stretch my unbandaged fingers to the palm
of my other hand. Every move my fingers make
is slow and careful.
But I stretch and practice.

Soon, I am ready for my old routine:
work until midnight at the chicken company;
in the early morning, shower and do my homework.
But my hand is not that quick.
I cut back to two shifts
but earn enough to buy the minutes and the food.

When it is June, Mrs. Mejía begins to prepare us
for final exams. Next year some of us will go into
mainstream classes.
I want to be one of them.

# Driving Lesson

When I look up, my mother turns away,
but I know she is sneaking looks at the pictures.
I sit in a spot of sun with the *Maine Department of
Motor Vehicles Driving Manual.*
I cannot tell her she should learn the rules of driving;
that would be too direct. Instead,
my mother sprawls in a chair by my side, peeking.
My mother stretches.
"What is that?" she says.
"It is stop," I say.
"Is red," she says.
"Wrong way," she says.
And then, "What is Wrong Way?"
"You can't drive in that direction," I answer.
"Turn around," she says.
"That's right," I say.
"Is that all?" she says.
I read, "If two cars come to an intersection
at the same time, yield to the car on your right."
"Yield."
"Let them go first," I say.
She shakes her head. "No. *You* go first.
They won't let you in. You will never get
on that road if you let them go first."
"Yes, you will. They cannot stop you," I say.
"It's the law."
She rises, walks in the kitchen waving her hand behind her.

She plugs in the kettle for tea. "More," she says.
I know she does not want to spin on the highway like Kadat.
"Bring me tea," she says, sitting back down.
I prepare two cups of tea with five sugars and milk.
When I return, her face is close to the pages
of the driving manual. I, too, sit on the couch.
We study Yield, Wrong Way, Do Not Enter,
Flashing Yellow, Red Light with a Green Arrow,
Blinking Red, School Zone.
"I am tired," my mother says.
I am exhausted.
My mother shuts her eyes.
I put down the driving manual.
We watch soaps from Cairo.
"You are a good teacher," my mother says.
I am *astonished* and *astounded* to hear this.
Vocabulary I learned from Mrs. Mejía.
Astonished.
Astounded.

# Braiding

We are all hanging out at Ezo, me and
Jackie, Poni, Lado, in the lull time
between lunch and dinner.
It's our first day of summer vacation.

I got my grades. All As. My friends are razzing me.
"You are the one they need in Sudan," Poni says,
"when independence comes."
"You are a top cream girl, V," Lado says.
I have a nickname, now. They call me V.
"The problem is my writing," I say.
I get no sympathy, since I read all of
*To Kill a Mockingbird* in one weekend.
We are silly. We girls sit on one side of the booth,
our arms wrapped around each other,
singing, "Lean on Me,"
roaring with laughter.
Poni says, "Hey girl, speaking of hair . . ."
"Who's speaking of hair?" Jackie says.
"Nobody says you got to braid your hair," Poni says.
She has put a little Bantu knot in mine.
"I vote for little crops.
And giant hoop earrings."
So we sing and talk about our hair like we
like to do, and who do you think should come in
but Lado's white friend,
the one who wants African braids.

Lado gets a smile that spreads across his cheeks.
"Now here's a girl needs some braids," he says.
"And here's a girl who owes me."
He nods to me.
"What have I done," I say, "to owe you?"
"You sulked around here for weeks, that's what."
The lady is blond.
Long, straight, blond hair.
"Jackie's the braider," I say.
She says, "Uh uh, not me."
I look out the window as if surely there is something
outside calling me away.
The lady says, "I have been waiting so long
to meet you." She shakes my hand.
Hers is so white. I remember Mrs. Mejía saying,
"You know how to braid." I stand up.
I must be two feet taller than Lado's friend's friend.
I take a few steps from our booth,
give myself some elbow room.
I sit the lady down on the floor with a
motion of my finger
the way Habuba used to do to me.
She is ecstatic, this girl.
I sit on the edge of a chair,
and she sits between my knees.
My fingers touch the fine, pale hair.
In my imagination
I put my fingers over my mother's.
Together, our fingers fly over the lady's hair
and we make a pattern, beginning at her crown

and moving down the back of her dainty head.
I am twisting the hair over and under.
The rhythm is natural in my fingers, and I remember
Kiden—my little cousin—and how she liked me
to do her hair and then she'd lean in to me
and flicker her eyelashes into mine. My fingers fly.
The rows are close to the white girl's head.
My fingers are not that strong yet,
but I give her twelve very narrow
braids down her scalp. They are not bad.
She is laughing. Jackie and Poni are cheering.
"You ought to get a job at Pierre's Beauty School,"
says the lady. Lado says, "I explained to her,
only if a girl grows up in Africa
can she do the African braids."
The blond lady, who looks better now
with her hair off her face, says,
"You could have a career doing braids."

After the lady is gone,
I stride past Lado, Poni, and Jackie
in the modeling gait Miss America Abby showed me.
"I could do hair in the morning," I say.
"And go to university in the afternoon."
Lado laughs.
"Why not?" I say sharply.
"Peace out, girl." Poni stares me down.
"Nobody can tell you what you will
or will not do."

We burst out laughing—because we have each other,
and at this moment
in the sun at Ezo's
we have what we want.

# When Peace Comes

In the summer, I work five days a week at Barber Foods.
Mostly I work and sleep.
On a lazy Sunday morning, Jackie and Poni braid
tiny micro braids in my hair, beginning
at the little hairs at the crown of my head.
"When peace comes, will you go home?" Jackie asks.
"Tomorrow—I will *go*," Poni says. "Very soon
we will reach the mountaintop in South Sudan."
"In Sudan you would have thirteen kids, Poni,
and be somebody's second wife," Jackie says.
I say, "Back home, we could not go to school.
But, you guys, I'd like to smell the dirt
on the banks of the Nile."
"*You guys*," they giggle. "Now she says, '*you guys*.'"
We all sigh and imagine the smells of beautiful Sudan.


In the long, quiet, sultry evening,
my mother and I borrow Frieda's car.
She has insurance now, a good thing
with my mother and me driving.
We drive down the road
where Andrew taught me to drive stick shift.
We practice parallel parking
so we can pass the driver's test.
We practice backing up in a straight line
and backing up in a loop.
"Do you remember Lokolumbe?" I ask my mother

when we are safely traveling forward.
"The boy in Cairo." While I drive,
my mother is filling out a Western Union
form to send money to a cousin now in Cairo.
We will put the form in the slot
at the Western Union office.
My mother says, "Yes, his mother is from Juba,
that boy Lokolumbe."
"Maybe someday we will bump into him at the
McDonald's on St. John Street," I say.
"Or maybe he is in Bismarck, North Dakota,
where he wanted to go."
My mother presses hard on her pen.
She does not look at me.
"The elders say we must"—she pauses—
"educate ourselves in American ways.
You are eighteen.
You can talk to that boy."
"Lokolumbe?"
"No, that boy."
My mother squints at the letter boxes on the form.
My hands cannot continue
and I pull over beside the U-Haul store.
I know his house.
I see his blue door.
"I am tired," my mother says.
"I go to work in one hour."
"He is a fisherman, like Habuba's father."
I feel the need to tell her.
"Drive me to the Western Union.

Then drive me home," she says.

"We will drive again tomorrow."

I drive, but my feet feel like they are dancing.

# Nine Times Out of Ten

"You look good. Go knock on his door.
He won't stand a chance," Jackie says.
"Forget him. He's a white boy," Poni says.
"Invite him for a walk," Abby says.
"If nothing's left between you . . . " She shrugs.
"I try to turn old boyfriends into friends.
Borrow Elsa. Everybody loves my dog."

For several days, I think of these ways
of talking to Andrew.
Poni's right. What good can come
from seeing a boy who's not in my tribe
or even African?
Then, I think, at least I could tell him
thank you for the day
I was a Russian girl with elephants.
Then Jackie comes in the door.
Kicks off her sneakers stained with sweet
mowed grass, slides down on a chair,
baseball cap over her braids.
"Hey, sister," she says.
"Just came from soccer practice.
Here's a message for *you*."
She hands me an envelope,
grabs her shoes, shouts,
"I'm late for work,"
and runs, barefoot, out my door.

The envelope is white.
The words on it are in a small,
black scrawl. I open it and
I read,

*Hey Viola,*
*Remember once you read a poem to me*
*about nirvana?*
*Something about nirvana being here,*
*nine times out of ten.*
*You told me it meant that nirvana*
*is some kind of good place in your head.*
*You need a friend, you know where I hang out,*
*down at the pier,*
*nine times out of ten.*
*Andrew*

# Elephant Trunk

The hot summer days are changing.
I feel a different kind of air on my skin.
Now and then I walk through the Old Port
but do not go down by the pier.
I wear an African skirt and T-shirt,
like I used to wear.
I have not seen Andrew for a long time.
I am at work most days.
But early one evening,
when the new school year is about to begin,
I keep walking
and come to the pier.
Andrew is working on his boat
as he said he would be,
at the end of the long fishing wharf.
Then I hear him call,
"Luck be my lady tonight!"
His voice carries over the wind.
He leaps up the skinny ladder
and over the pilings.
I almost run away but do not.
"Viola," he yells.
He was never shy.
I have not seen him in so long,
but I know more things about him.
I know his mom is sick with alcohol,
and he helps his family pay the bills.
Like I do.

He is running. He wears a baseball cap,
and I cannot see the red hair.
The temperature is cool.
A pink sun is descending to the ocean.
Rays from the disappearing sun streak the sky.
In the alleyway a fisherman hauls up crates of lobster.
Andrew bends toward me, hands in his pockets,
grinning and speechless, shaking his head,
his green eyes teary in the wind.
Soon the moon will hang
just over the buildings in the Old Port.
"Let's take a spin around the bay,"
Andrew says.
I shrug. "I could," I say.
I step down a long ladder into the boat.

The sea shines with buoys and lights.
Andrew works the controls, soon the engine catches,
and we zigzag past boats in the harbor.
From the wheelhouse,
we watch the city of lights come on,
and I know this moon is the moon Gwendolyn sees
and Francis and I imagined we climbed to.
I feel the surge of the boat over the water.
"See that star formation?" Andrew says.
I look up where Andrew is pointing
and see a stream of stars.
"It's called the Elephant's Trunk," he says.
We both look at the sky. It is aglitter.
"In Khartoum," I tell Andrew,

"the Blue Nile and the White Nile
come together like this."
I touch the fingers of one hand to the
bent elbow of my other arm.
"That's what Khartoum means—
it means Elephant's Trunk,
the shape the two rivers make
when they meet."
I remember Habuba making the shape
of the elephant's trunk with her arms
for one of her many stories.
Andrew's grinning at me.
We pick up speed in the open bay.
"I like being up so high!" I call to him over the wind.
"Did you have to sneak over here?" he calls back.
"No. It's okay," I say.
He is looking for something in my eyes or my face.
"What's this?" he says. He sees
my extensions falling down my back.
"Poni and Jackie did these."
Salt water sprays my face.
I am drenched, and laugh,
and sop the water with my skirt.
He can see my hand for himself, even that I
painted my fingernails like Mrs. Mejía's.
We circle the bay. I wish I could see his red hair.
I tell him I've been studying the driving manual
and last week I passed the test. I want to say,
would you take off your cap so I can look at your hair?
He says he's got a job on this guy's boat. He'll be

working weekends, mostly. He can hang out more
at school, maybe even graduate this year.
"I missed you," he says, tossing me a towel.
The wind whips my braids.
I look at him. I am soggy and laughing.
"Sweet," I say.
The boat pounds through the waves,
and I love the feel of its power.
I reach my arms up and shout *hallooo*
to the elephant's trunk in the sky.

# Three Brothers

On my way walking from the pier,
I pass a bookstore. It is lit and open,
and I step in.
The man at the desk is wearing a straw hat
and beside him is a little dog he calls Charlotte.
"Charlotte," he tells me, "is ready for dinner."
She has her own bowl of water and a cushion.
I ask him, "Do you have a book by Walter Mosley?"
"Excellent choice." The clerk and Charlotte
show me a shelf full of books by Mr. Mosley.
I pick out one called *White Butterfly*. The man slides
it into a paper bag, and that's how I'll mail it
to Lokolumbe at the Church of the Sudanese.
I picture his hands turning the package
this way and that. I will tell him
my American story. He may no longer be
at the Church of the Sudanese,
but he is a boy from Juba, and we will find him.
I walk back to my mother in the cool air with
the book. I remember my brothers,
the boy with the narrow back,
Francis in the Magic Kingdom T-shirt,
and Lokolumbe offering me the desert
with the sweep of his arm.
*For this moment, let's be free,* I say to them.
They could not know the dance
of the journey I am just beginning,
but they dance with me always.

# Girl from Juba

My mother has made friends with the caseworker.
She cooks moto-moto and sambusas for her.
The caseworker brought my mother a chocolate layer cake.
Andrew came by, and we ate slices
as big as one of Habuba's kisras.
Now Frieda comes and goes. We like having her and Jamal,
and no matter what, they will stay, sharing my room.
Charles, our neighbor, comes sometimes for the news
from Cairo. But he is studying now at the university
and stays only a while, shakes our hands, and leaves.

The nights have gotten longer.
I sit on the couch beside my mother with Jamal,
a solid, warm weight plopped
in my lap. He is singing the names of
animals he looks at in a picture book.
Out the window the moon is shining.
My mother tells me to sit on the floor.
I do with Jamal still in my lap,
and her strong fingers
begin to massage jojoba oil into my hair.
Jamal holds the book high in the air,
then drops his head back against my belly,
grinning upside down at me.
"Who is this boy," I tease,
"this one who eats Cocoa Puffs for breakfast?"
I scoop him up the way Habuba would have.
I play the traditional game. "Who wants this child?

Anybody want this child?" and pretend to pass him
around to Frieda or my mother while he squeals.
My mother describes for him
the feel of the earth when the elephants walk,
and Jamal's eyes grow wide.
I shut my eyes and can feel the heat
of the cook fire in our courtyard.
Then comes a hint of the smell
of the earth by the Nile.
I'm an American girl in Portland, Maine.
But I am also
a girl from Juba.

# Historical Note

Three books in particular provided background for my writing: Ryszard Kapuściński's *The Shadow of the Sun*, Scott Peterson's *Me Against My Brother*, and Ngũgĩwa Thiong'o's *A Grain of Wheat*. These writers all explore effects of European colonialism in Africa.

The borders of many nations, including Sudan, were arbitrarily drawn by imperial powers. Sudan's British colonizers united two regions that had a long history of hostility—southern Sudan, whose people identify with African cultures and practice tribal faiths and Christianity, and northern Sudan, whose people are mostly Muslim and identify with Arab cultures.

Sudan achieved independence from Britain in 1956, but armed conflict between the north and south followed for sixteen years, until 1972. After the discovery of oil in southern Sudan, the regime of the north fought to force their culture on the culture of the south. In 1983, after the government of the north imposed strict Islamic law on the non-Muslim south, many southern tribes united to form the Sudan People's Liberation Army under John Garang. They fought to maintain their culture and African identity. In this tragic conflict, the longest war in the history of Africa and a war that the world has called genocide, an estimated 2 million people, mostly women and children, were killed.

In 2005, the Sudanese president Omar al-Bashir and the rebel leader John Garang signed the Comprehensive Peace Accord, bringing an end to direct conflict and agreeing that in five years, the people of the south would vote in a referendum to either unite with northern Sudan or become an independent nation. In January 2011, nearly 99 percent of the people of the south voted for independence. On July 9, 2011, the nation of South Sudan was born.

In 2009, the International Criminal Court (ICC) at The Hague issued a warrant of arrest for al-Bashir for continued atrocities against civilians in Sudan's western region of Darfur. He was charged with war crimes, crimes against humanity, and genocide. The ICC issued a second warrant of arrest in 2010. In 2011, fighting broke out between the Army of Sudan and rebels in South Kordofan and Blue Nile, two states near the border between Sudan and South Sudan.

Before coming to the United States, Viola and her family traveled over 1,730 miles from Juba, in what is now South Sudan, through northern Sudan to Wadi Halfa, then to Aswan, Egypt, and, finally, Cairo. South Sudan, as represented here, became an independent nation on July 9, 2011.

# Acknowledgments

Although this novel is based on events in the recent history of Sudan, *The Good Braider* is a work of fiction. Each of the characters is a fictional creation, but the Sudanese community of Portland, Maine—one of the largest Sudanese communities in the United States—is vibrant and real.

I was able to gain some understanding of this community after a family from southern Sudan welcomed me into their Kennedy Park home in Portland and into their lives. Thomas William was the first member of the family I met, shortly after he came to the United States. It was from Thomas that I heard the phrase "If you eat alone, it is as if you have not eaten." He was describing how difficult it was for his family to be scattered and living in different places.

I experienced good times and hard times with his sister, Suzan William, and many of her friends, all students at Portland High during the years I was researching this novel. They told me stories of the war, introduced me to Congolese music, shared the art of hair braiding, and once, after everybody got off work, we cooked all night for a graduation party.

Oliver Lomeri talked with me many days as we walked through Portland. He told me his memories of how difficult it was to go to school and of his family's separation when they tried to leave Sudan.

Florence Olebe told me about her experience of coming to Maine with her seven sons and opening an African restaurant in Portland. Her restaurant, Ezo African

Restaurant, is an actual restaurant that is no longer open but had many shining years on Oak Street and served as a cultural bridge between the city's new African residents and longtime Mainers. Thank you, Jane, Ben, Ludia, Sabi, Frieda, Dominick, Stella, Winnie, Josephine—all of South Sudan and Portland, Maine—for the years and stories we shared.

A conversation with Ed Willett, former head of the Portland High School Civil Rights Team, stayed with me as I wrote. He told me about the careful, tense, and courageous conversations at Portland High among Muslim students, Christian students, and students of other faiths, and about the work on the part of many to create a safe place in the school for all. He was proud of his own Irish immigrant background, one of the "rowdies, who came off the hill," he said, referring to one of Portland's immigrant neighborhoods. He saw many parallels between new refugees and Portland's earlier immigrants. I'm grateful to Mr. Willett, and to the many teachers both in Portland, Maine, and Manchester, New Hampshire, who shared their experiences with me.

Rashida Mohamed, a Victim/Witness Advocate with the Manchester, New Hampshire, Police Department and from Khartoum, Sudan, gave critically important comments on the novel. We discussed the hardships endured by the Muslim people of northern Sudan during the long years of the civil war and also talked about the politics of color and race. Other readers were invaluable to me: James Deng of South Sudan and Portland, Maine; Katie Nye, Office of Refugees and Immigrants, Boston, Massachusetts; Lydia DeLorey and Aleris Dilligaf, my transcultural friends, and the organization Amesbury for Africa.

Thank you to my early readers, Lucy Honig, the poet Susan Roney O'Brian, and Susan's class of young writers at Thomas Prince Middle School in Princeton, Massachusetts. Thank you to Rodger Martin and my sustaining colleagues of the Monadnock Poets, John Mort, and photographer Kate Philbrick. Thank you, Tracey Adams of Adams Literary for your faith. Cindy Lord and Toni Buzzeo were readers and friends throughout. Their feedback was vital. My editor, Melanie Kroupa, asked me questions that opened the world to me as a writer, and I thank her, and Sharon McBride, for bringing such vision and care to this story.

I have had the opportunity to work with refugee families from many countries. Sometimes they have asked me to write down their stories so they won't be lost. Many young people, as well as elders, who came to the U.S. as refugees are now telling and writing their own stories. To you new storytellers, I pass on the words of another teller, Barry Lopez:

> *The stories people tell have a way of taking care of them. If stories come to you, care for them. And learn to give them away where they are needed.*

*"There is no word," the boy said to me, trying to describe his native foods. "My mother will cook it for you."*

—Terry Farish's journal, 2001

The boy's mother did cook it for her, and that was the beginning of Terry's long journey into the stories of new Americans from Sudan.

Terry Farish has written a number of books, including *Flower Shadows* about the Vietnam War which *Kirkus Reviews* describes as "a story as moving as it is wise." She taught writing at the Salt Institute for Documentary Studies and has recorded oral histories with people from Sudan, Vietnam, Cambodia, and other countries from which people have fled due to war and ethnic violence. She now directs the New Hampshire Humanities Council literacy program that serves many immigrants and refugees. Ms. Farish lives in Portsmouth, New Hampshire.